I took up sculpture because what interested me in painting was a clarification of my ideas. I changed my method, and worked in clay in order to have a rest from painting where I had done all I could for the time being. That is to say that it was done for the purposes of organization, to put order into my feelings, and find a style to suit me. When I found it in sculpture, it helped me in my painting. It was always in view of a complete possession of my mind, a sort of hierarchy of all my sensations, that I kept working in the hope of finding an ultimate method. HENRI MATISSE[1]

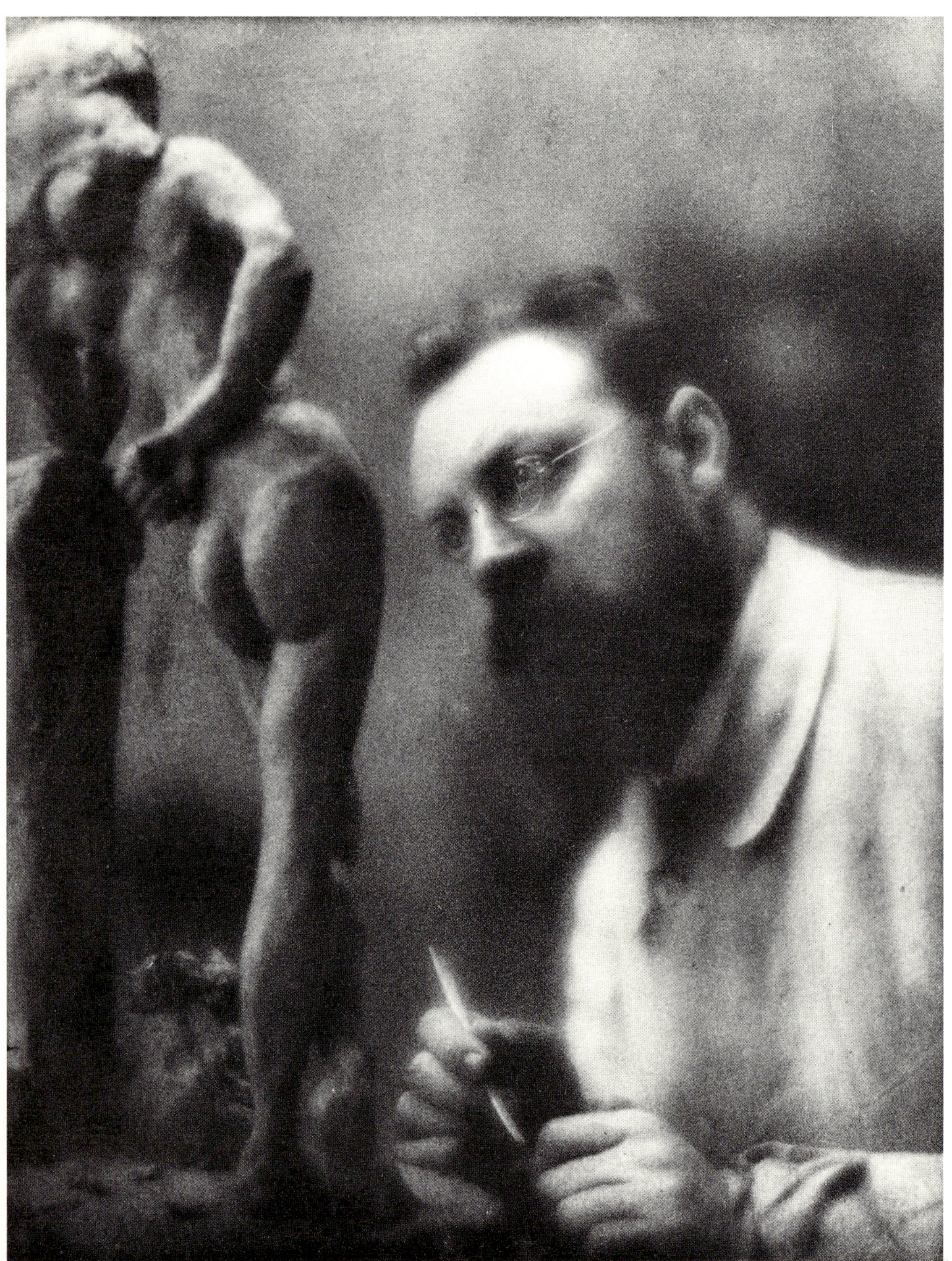

Alicia Legg

THE SCULPTURE OF MATISSE

The Museum of Modern Art, New York

Trustees of The Museum of Modern Art

Library of Congress Catalog Card Number 73-188667
ISBN 0-87070-448-6

Designed by James Wageman
Printed in the United States of America

The Museum of Modern Art
11 West 53 Street, New York, N.Y. 10019

Schedule of the Exhibition:

The Museum of Modern Art, New York
February 24–May 8, 1972

Walker Art Center, Minneapolis
June 20–August 6, 1972

University Art Museum, University of California, Berkeley
September 18–October 29, 1972

Front and back covers: *La Serpentine*. 1909.
Frontispiece: Edward Steichen. *Henri Matisse (and "La Serpentine"), Issy-les-Moulineaux*. 1909.
The Museum of Modern Art, New York.

Contents

Lenders to the Exhibition

Mr. and Mrs. James S. Adams, Dr. and Mrs. Harry Bakwin, Mr. and Mrs. Walter Bareiss, Mr. and Mrs. Sidney F. Brody, Harry I. Caesar, Mr. and Mrs. Ralph F. Colin, Mr. and Mrs. Nathan Cummings, Mr. and Mrs. Richard S. Davis, Mr. and Mrs. Lee V. Eastman, Mr. and Mrs. Allan D. Emil, Joseph H. Hirshhorn Collection, Mr. and Mrs. Paul Kantor, Mr. and Mrs. Fritz Katz, Mrs. Melville J. Kolliner, Mrs. M. Victor Leventritt, Mrs. Philip N. Lilienthal, The Jeffrey H. Loria Collection, Lewis Manilow, Jean Matisse, Pierre Matisse, Frank Perls, Nelson A. Rockefeller, Florene M. Schoenborn and Samuel A. Marx Collection, Mrs. Bertram Smith, Mr. and Mrs. Edward M. M. Warburg, Joy S. Weber, Mr. and Mrs. Benjamin Weiss, Mr. and Mrs. Howard A. Weiss

The Baltimore Museum of Art; The Art Institute of Chicago; Weatherspoon Art Gallery, The University of North Carolina at Greensboro; Los Angeles County Museum of Art; The Metropolitan Museum of Art, New York; The Minneapolis Institute of Arts; The Museum of Modern Art, New York; Musée Matisse, Nice; The Philip H. and A. S. W. Rosenbach Foundation, Philadelphia; San Francisco Museum of Art; Stanford University Museum of Art, Stanford, California

Robert Elkon Gallery, New York

Acknowledgments

It is a pleasure to express my appreciation, and that of the Trustees of The Museum of Modern Art; the Walker Art Center, Minneapolis; and the University Art Museum, University of California, Berkeley to the Matisse family for their cooperation in the preparation of this exhibition. The artist's daughter, Madame Georges Duthuit, and sons, Jean Matisse and Pierre Matisse have been patient and understanding in replying to frequent requests for information and generous in providing loans. Very special thanks are owed to the lenders — collectors, museums, and galleries — whose names are listed on page 6, as well as those who wish to remain anonymous. The advice and assistance of Frank Perls and Pierre Schneider have been extremely helpful. Others who have aided in locating works and securing loans are Mrs. Ilse Gerson, Mrs. Cynthia McCabe, Abram Lerner, and B. C. Holland. Two Matisse scholars whose works have led to my own discoveries are Alfred H. Barr, Jr., and Albert E. Elsen. Mr. Barr's book, *Matisse: His Art and His Public*, continuously reveals new aspects of this great twentieth-century master; Professor Elsen made valuable suggestions, and was kind enough to give me access to the manuscript and photographs for his forthcoming book, *The Sculpture of Henri Matisse.*

The collaboration of many Museum departments is essential in a project of this nature, and the help of staff members too numerous to mention is gratefully acknowledged. Among my colleagues whose interest and support have been invaluable are William S. Lieberman who first proposed the show a number of years ago; Helen M. Franc, William S. Rubin, and Kynaston McShine, whose suggestions for the text were constructive and imaginative; and Harriet Schoenholz Bee, who edited this publication. Others to whom I am indebted are Cora Rosevear, for research and help with the installation; Jane Adlin, for the varied secretarial work that goes into the preparation of an exhibition and catalogue; Judith Di Meo, for French translations; Jean-Edith Weiffenbach, for arranging the transportation of the works, and recording them; Charles Froom, Production Supervisor, for advice, and his associates for executing the many steps in all phases of the exhibition's installation.

Alicia Legg, *Director of the Exhibition*

Profile of a Woman. 1894. 9⅝″ d.

Profile of a Woman. 1894. 9⅝″ d.

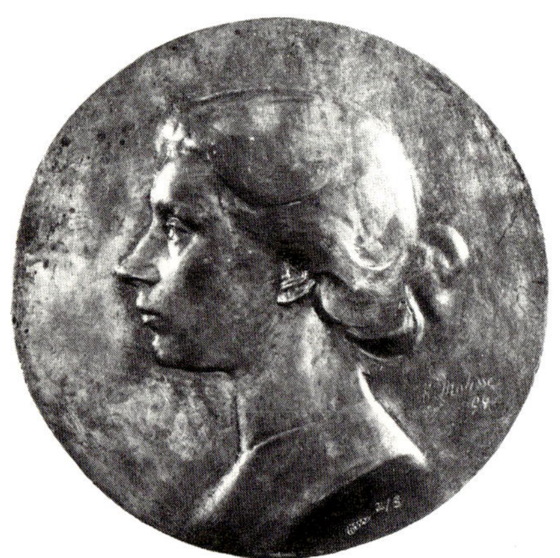

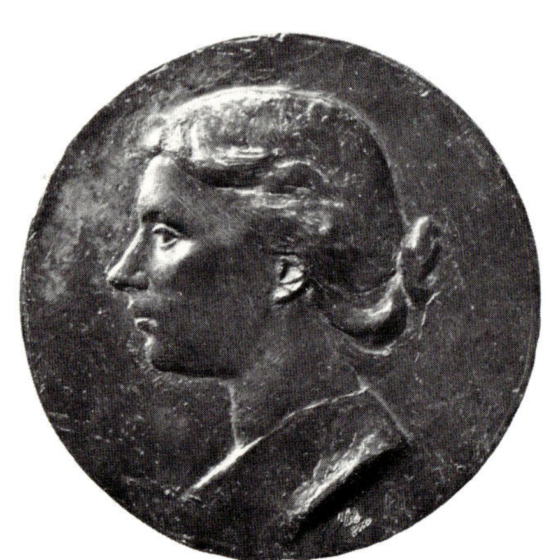

Copy after Barye's *Jaguar Devouring a Hare*. 1899–1901. 9″ h.

Study of a Foot. 1900. 11¾″ h.

Horse. 1901. 6¾″ h.

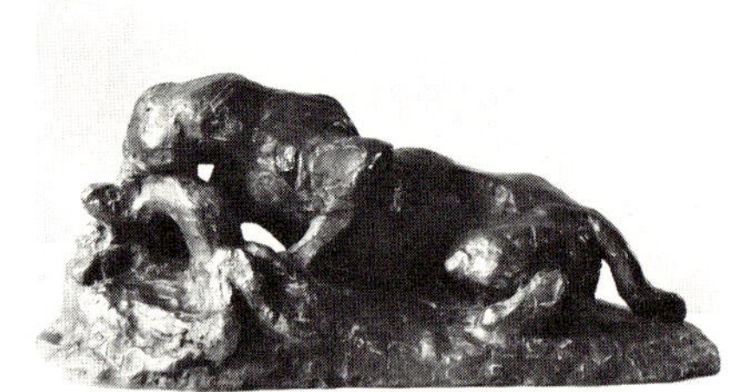

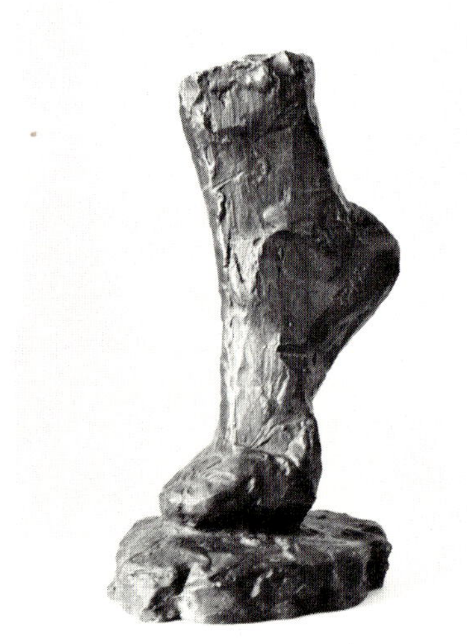

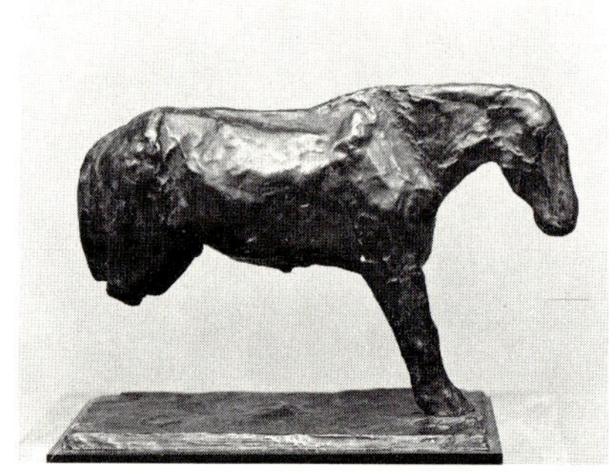

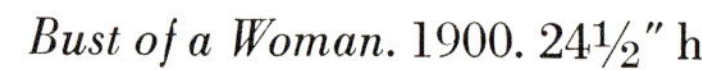

Bust of a Woman. 1900. 24½″ h.

Copy after Puget's *Ecorché*. 1903. 9″ h.

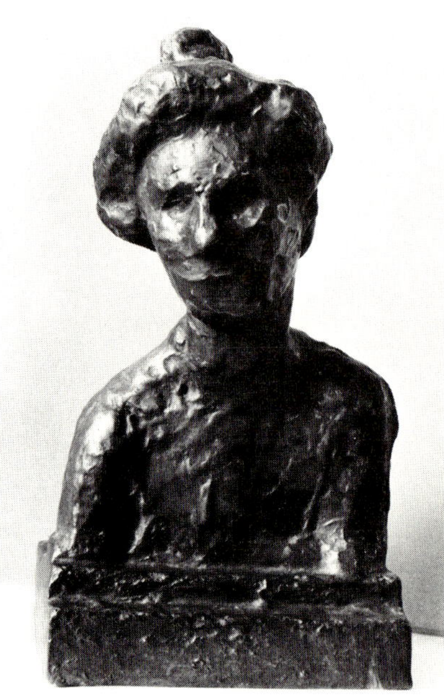

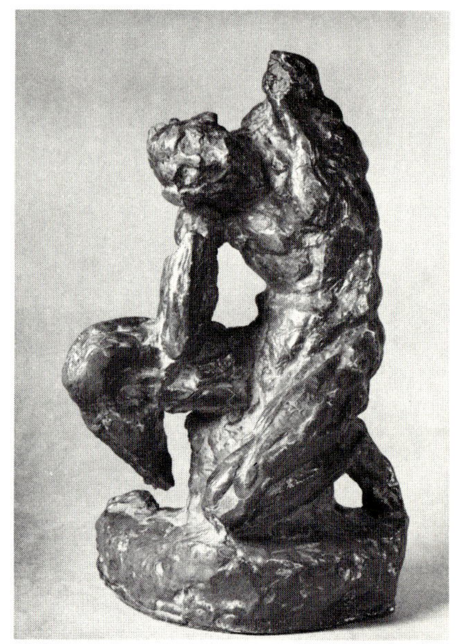

The Sculpture of Matisse

The first Matisse exhibition devoted primarily to sculpture was held in 1912 at Alfred Stieglitz's Photo-Secession Gallery in New York. The following year, *The Back, I,* 1909, was included in the "Armory Show" and since that time, examples of his more important sculptures have been seen periodically in New York and other principal American cities. During the 1950s, a number of important exhibitions of Matisse's sculpture were held.[2] One of these showings, at the Kunsthaus, Zurich, in 1959, was virtually complete—all but two of the sixty-nine known bronzes and one carved-wood piece were represented. The present exhibition includes all the bronzes and some related drawings and prints, bringing to the United States for the first time the full range of Matisse as a sculptor.[3]

Henri-Emile-Benoît Matisse was born December 31, 1869, at Le Cateau-Cambrésis (Nord). He was preparing for a career in law when, in 1891, he decided to become an artist and went to Paris to enter the class of Adolphe William Bouguereau at the Académie Julian. Soon disillusioned with academic instruction, he gained admission to the studio of Gustave Moreau at the Ecole des Beaux-Arts. Moreau's liberal attitude and encouragement of individual expression stimulated Matisse; Moreau also introduced him to the masters at the Louvre, whom he studied and copied. He had little formal training as a sculptor; in 1899 he attended evening sessions in sculpture at the Ecole de la Ville de Paris, and after failing to interest Auguste Rodin in some of his drawings, he worked for several months with Rodin's leading pupil, Antoine Bourdelle, at the studios of La Grande Chaumière.

Although Matisse's first known sculptures (of 1894) are a pair of bas-relief portraits of a young woman in profile, the influences of Rodin and Antoine-Louis Barye, the eminent animal sculptor, are evident in his first efforts at freestanding modeling. Among these is a free copy of Barye's *Jaguar Devouring a Hare* (completed in 1901) in which the tense drama of the original is captured almost as if in shorthand. This improvisational effect is misleading, however, in light of the fact that Matisse worked for two years on this piece and studied the animal's anatomy extensively. Rodin's influence is also apparent in *Study of a Foot* and *Bust of a Woman,* both of 1900, a small *Horse* of 1901, and another free copy, this one of the standard studio prop, Puget's *Ecorché* (1903), the male figure whose flayed skin leaves bare its muscular structure.[4]

Of another and more celebrated sculpture, *The Serf,* 1900–03, it is said that there were over a hundred sittings with the model Bevilaqua, who had posed in 1877 for Rodin's *Walking Man.* Rodin's youthful, striding figure has matured in Matisse's *Serf,* whose widespread muscular legs are firmly rooted to the base. The arms were cut off above the elbows before the work was cast, giving more emphasis to the forward thrust of the brooding head and protruding abdomen. "Matisse worked laboriously . . . a sculpture which sprang from a conception close to that of Rodin, became something else, more rugged and partially misshapen, but extremely expressive."[5]

During this period, Matisse completed two female figures; in *Madeleine, I,* 1901, the rhythmic line of his early drawings and paintings of the nude model is carried further than in the conventional studio poses. The eye is led from the foot to the head along an unbroken

The Serf. 1900–03. $37\frac{3}{8}$" h.

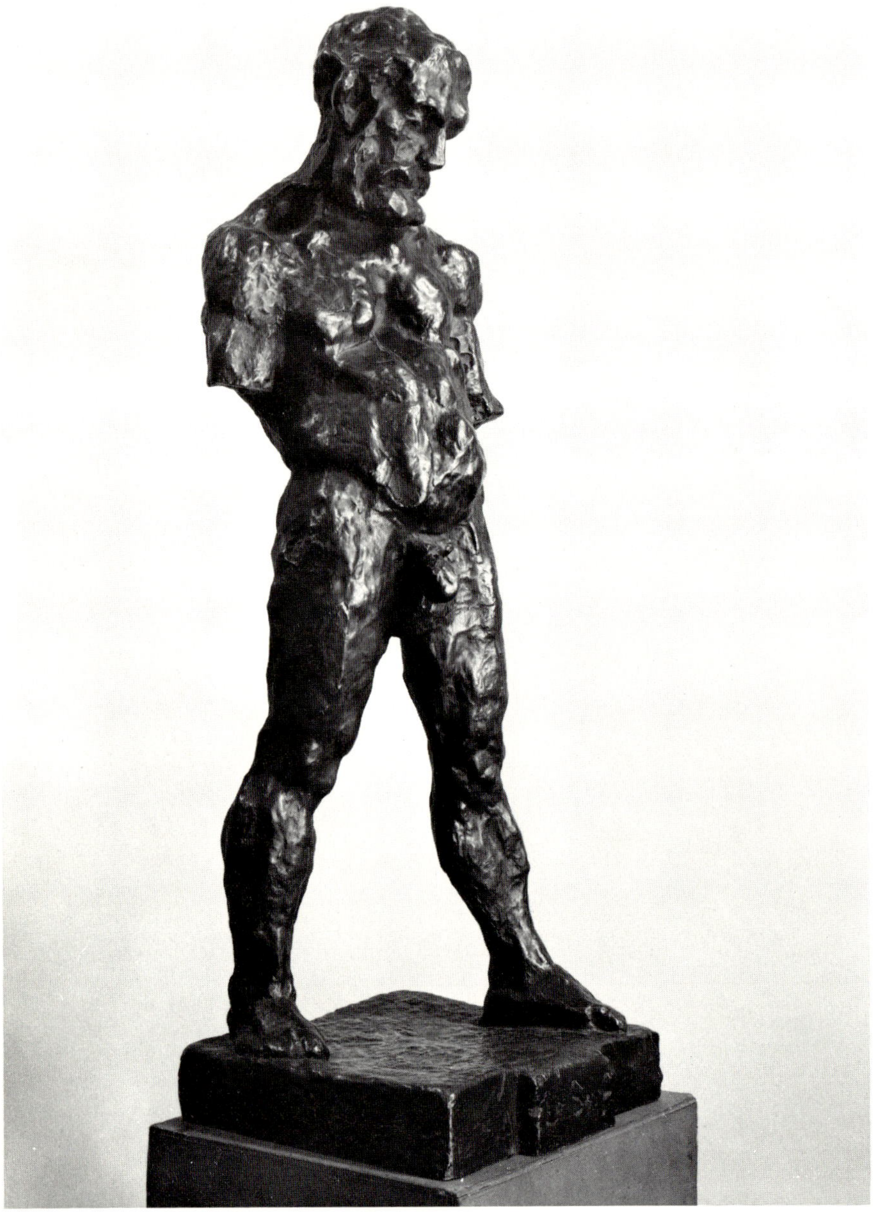

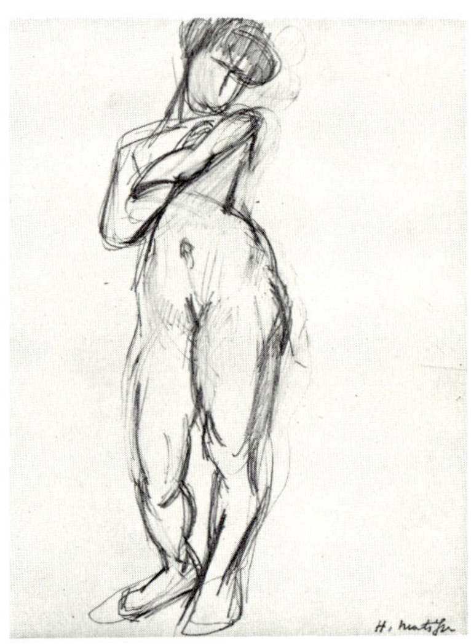

Study for *Madeleine.*
ca. 1901. Pencil

Madeleine, I. 1901. 23⅜" h.

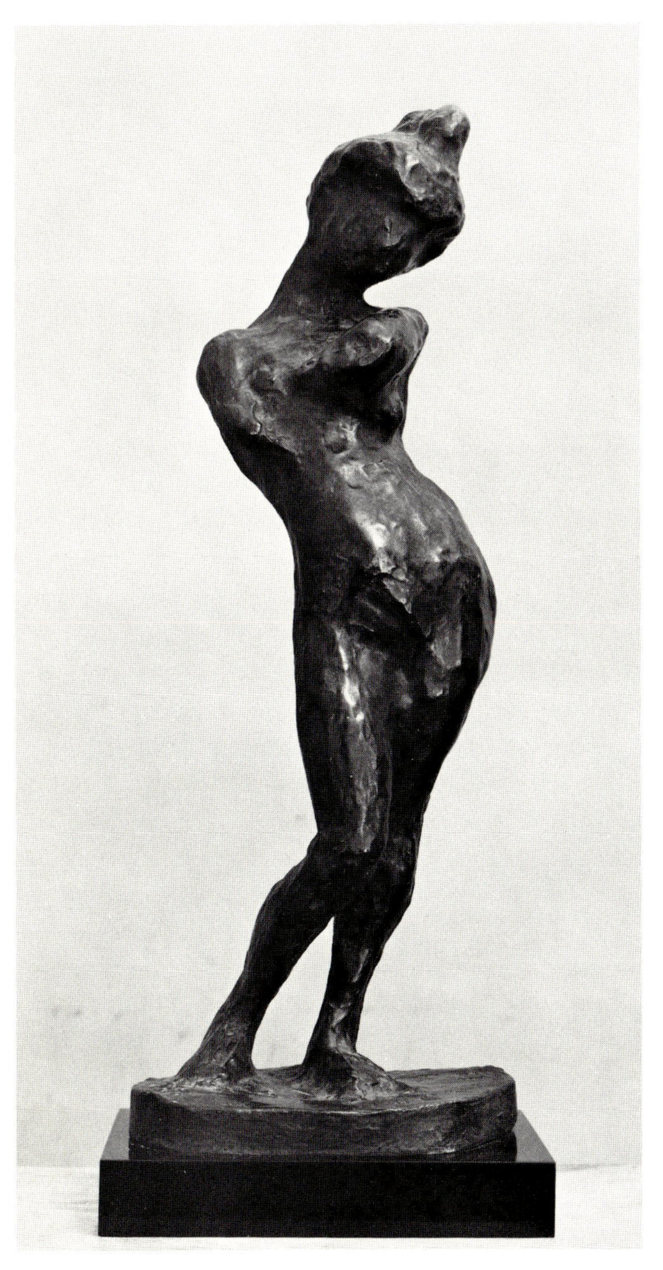

Madeleine, II. 1903. 23⅞" h.

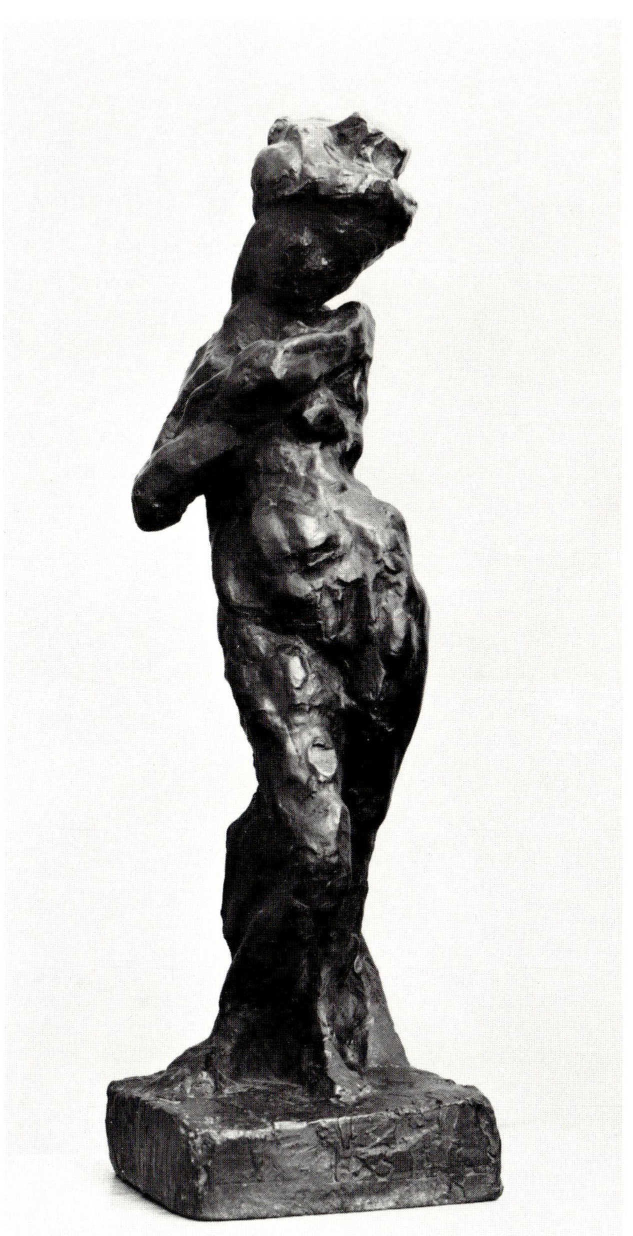

Seated Nude with Arms on Head. 1904. $13\frac{7}{8}$" h.

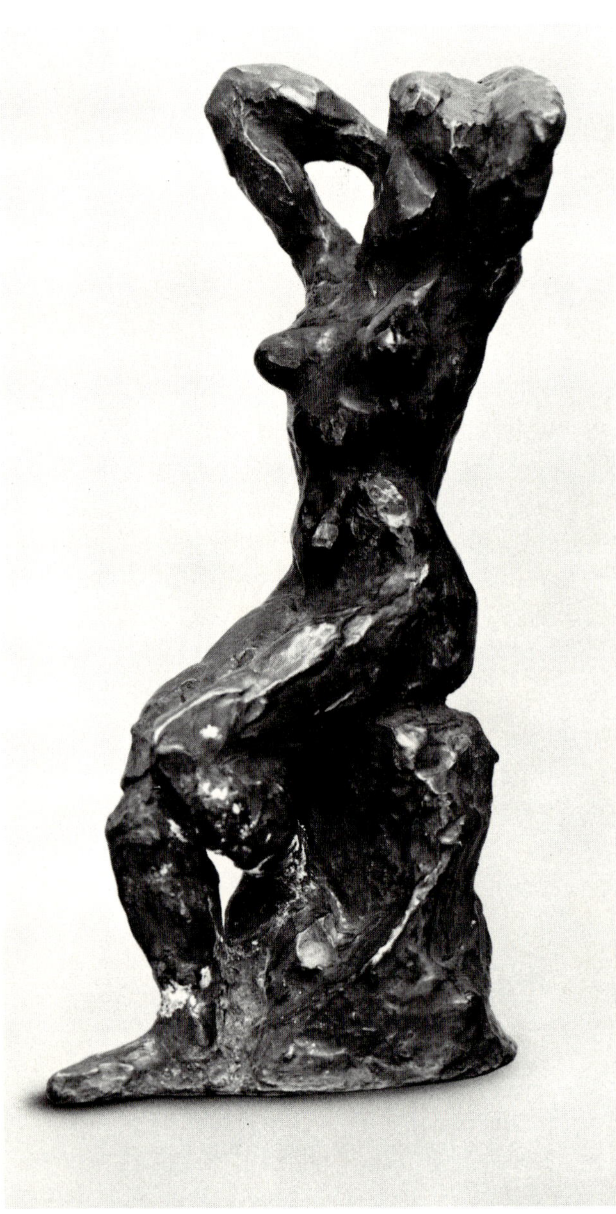

flowing curve (the folded arms are barely suggested) that imparts a languid grace to the figure. The same pose is used in *Madeleine, II*, 1903, with its animated, broken surface in contrast to the smooth modeling of the earlier version. Here the arms are folded across the chest, and the torso is vibrant with life and movement.

In painting, Matisse had done some pictures in the Impressionist style, had studied Turner and Cézanne, and through Signac, knew the doctrine of Pointillism. His own style emerged in 1905 when, along with artists of his own generation, André Derain, Maurice Vlaminck, Albert Marquet, and others, he sent some paintings to the Salon d'Automne. The sensation caused by the violent colors and bold brushwork of these artists caused a critic to call them "Fauves" or "wild beasts." Matisse's paintings of this time, *Luxe, calme et volupté*, 1904–05, and the celebrated *Joy of Life*, 1906, include figures in poses that were to become the classic repertory in his sculpture—the reclining nude, the upright figure with one knee bent, the crouching figure, and the gesture of arms raised above the head as if arranging the hair.

During the Fauve period, Matisse completed a number of small figures and heads. Notable among the figures is *Torso with Head (La Vie)*, 1906, in which the arch of the back is exaggerated and the truncated arms are raised like sprouting wings; the small pointed breasts and jutting buttocks recall African Negro sculpture, which Matisse was among the first to know and admire. Among the heads are the tiny relief of 1903 of his daughter Marguerite, and the 1905 heads of two small boys, his son Pierre and the son of the painter

Upright Nude with Arched Back. 1904. 8⅞″ h.

Torso with Head (La Vie). 1906. 9⅛″ h.

Standing Nude, Arms on Head. 1906. 10⅜″ h.

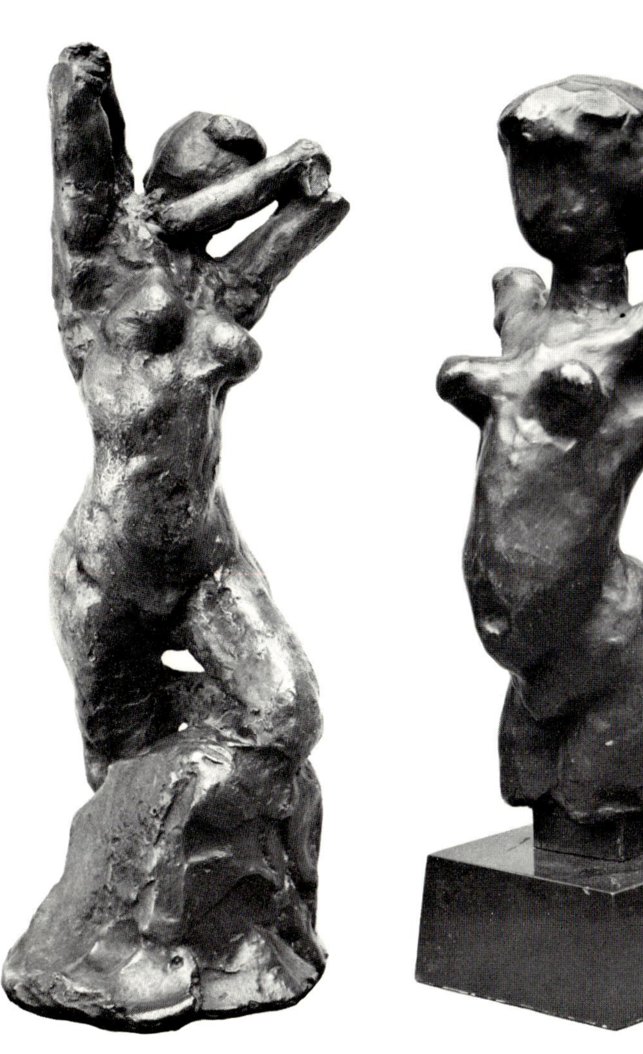

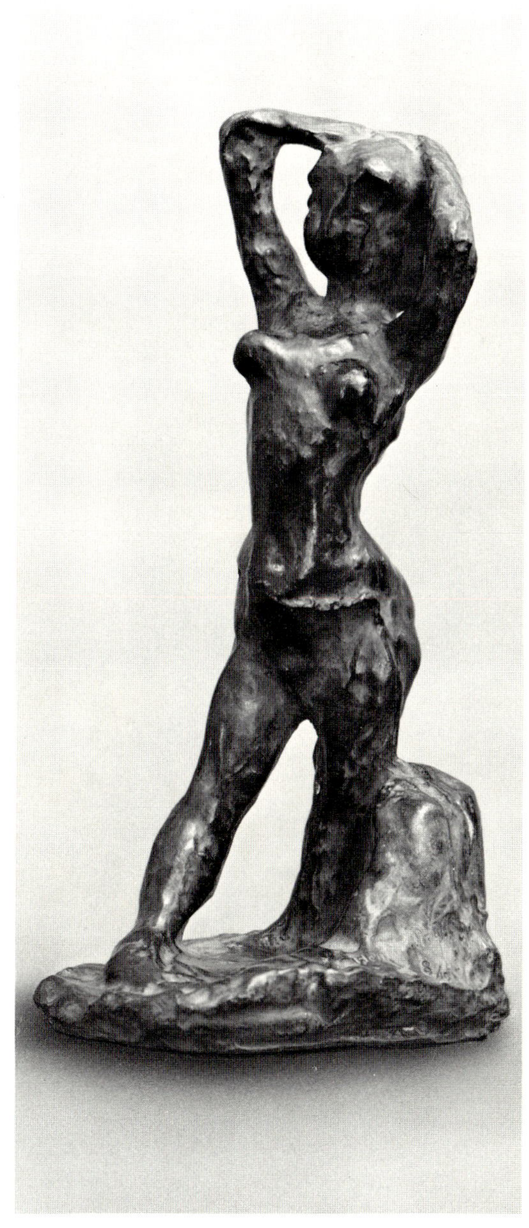

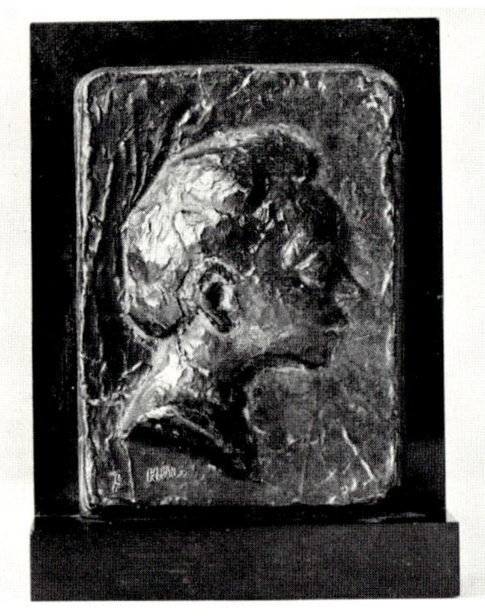
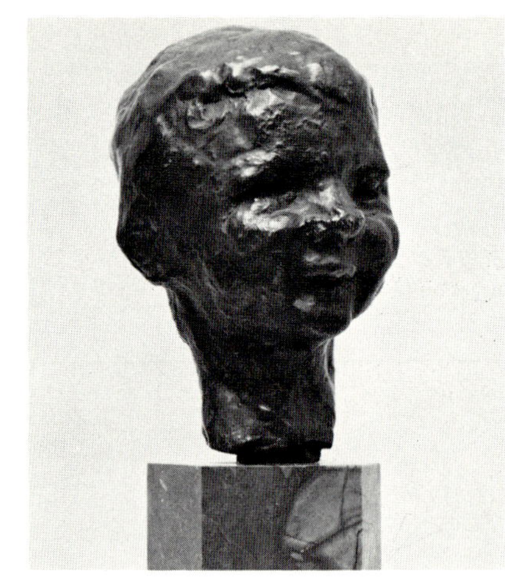
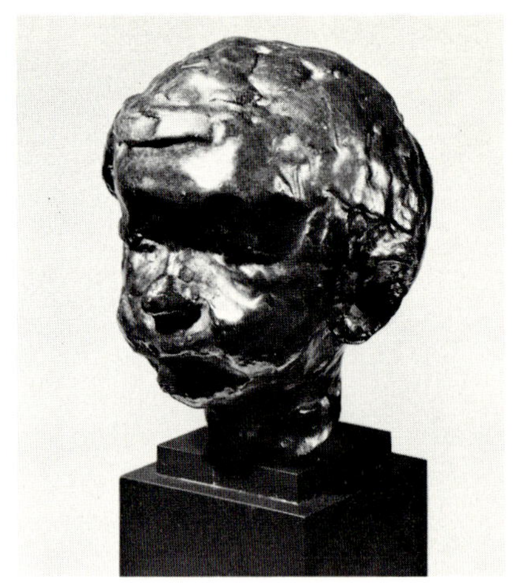
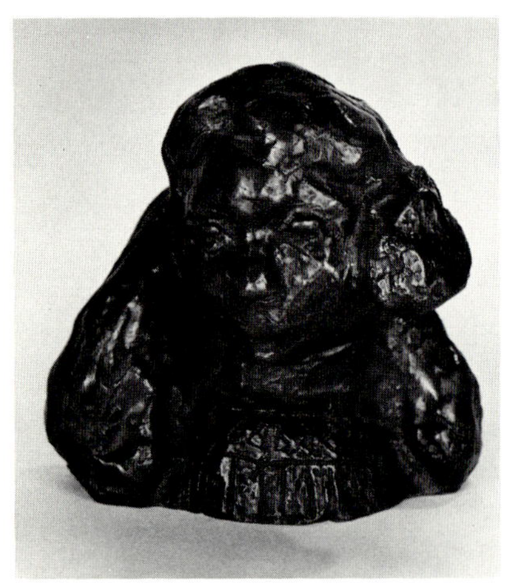
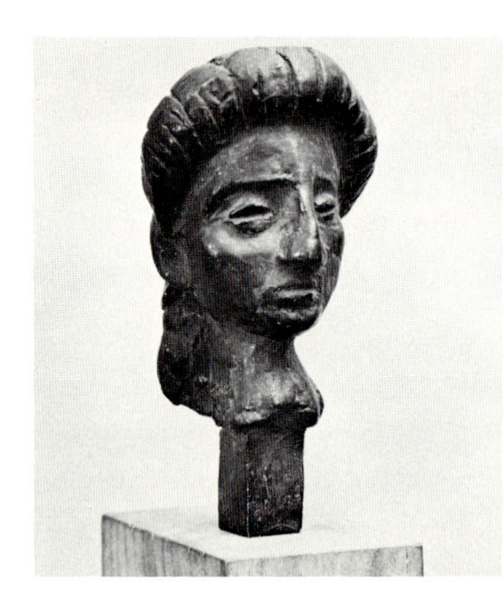
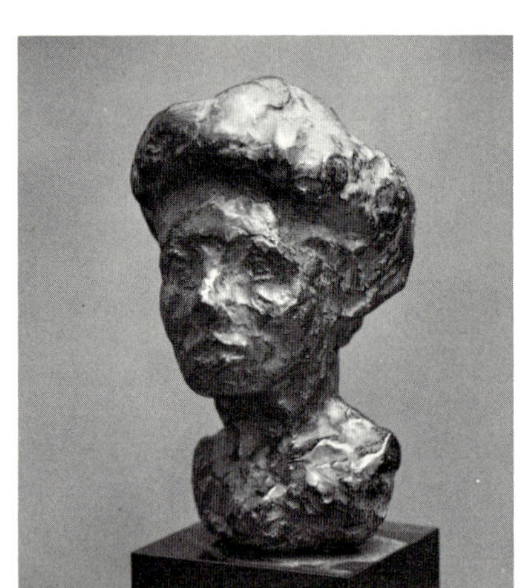
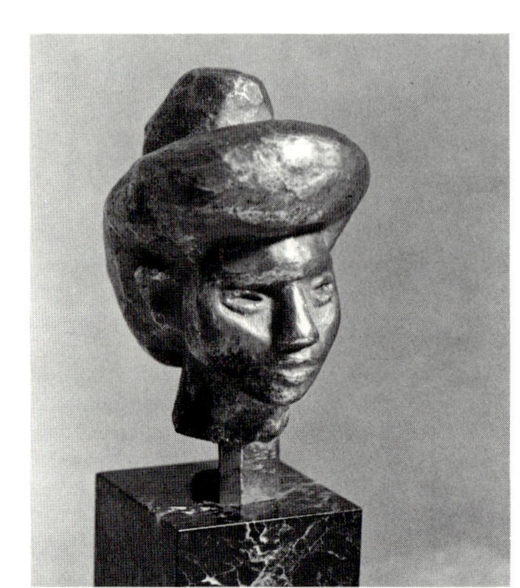
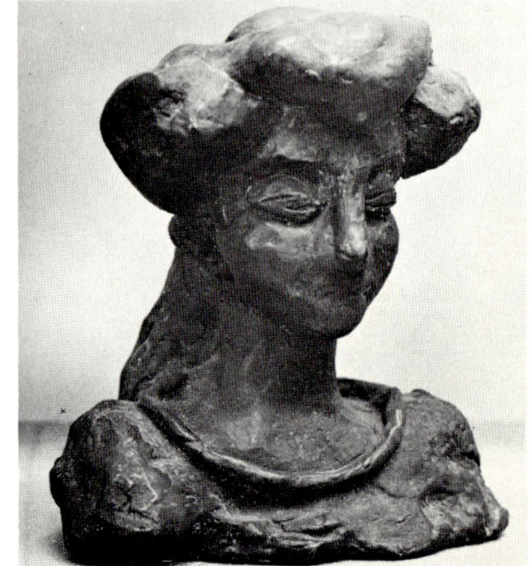

FACING PAGE:

Profile of a Child (Marguerite). 1903. 5″ h.

Head of a Child (Pierre Matisse). 1905. 6 3/8″ h.

Head of a Child (Pierre Manguin). 1905. 5 1/8″ h.

Head of a Young Girl (Marguerite). 1906. 6 1/4″ h.

Small Head with Upswept Hair. 1906. 4 1/2″ h.

Small Head with Flat Nose. 1906. 6 1/4″ h.

Small Head with Comb. 1907. 3 3/4″ h.

Head with Necklace. 1907. 5 7/8″ h.

THIS PAGE:

Thorn Extractor. 1906. 7 1/2″ h.

Head of a Faun. 1907. 5 1/2″ h.

Rosette. 1905. 4 1/4″ h.

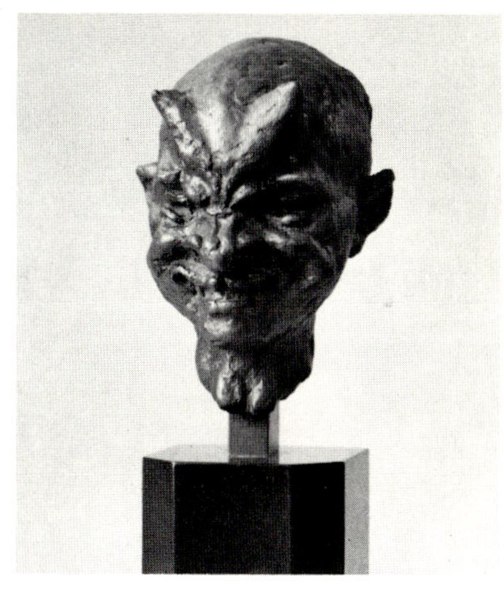

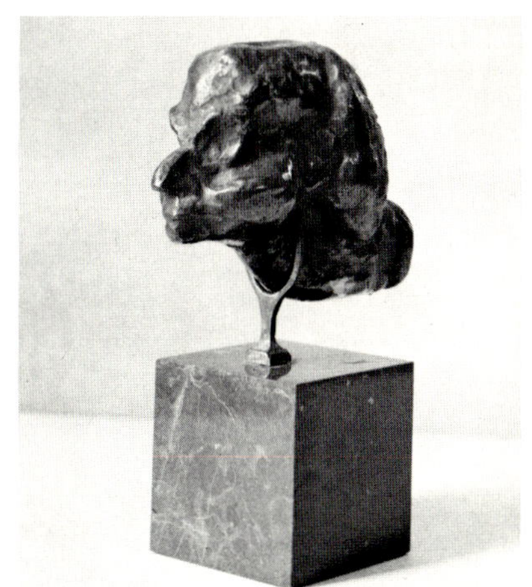

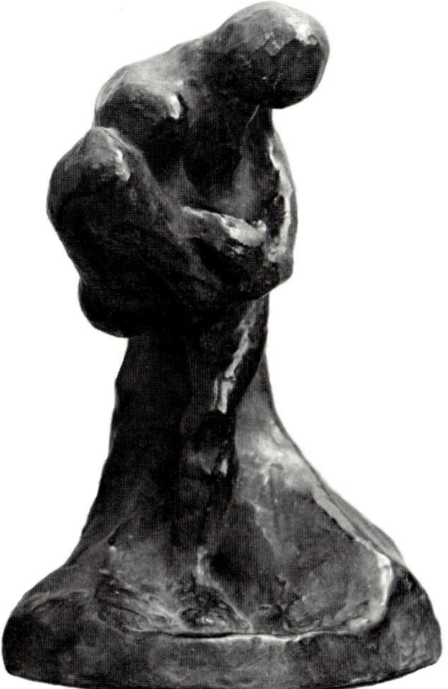

Woman Leaning on Her Hands. 1905. 5¼" h.

Manguin. In these he captures the characteristic personality of each child. In 1906 and 1907, seven small but expressive heads were created. Two of the most compelling are *Small Head with Upswept Hair*, with its aquiline features and hair rolled in the Greek style and *Small Head with Comb* which is modeled in the classic manner.

Also of this period are a number of sculptures that testify to Matisse's mastery of the figure in relation to its space; among these are the small seated *Woman Leaning on Her Hands* of 1905, a complex arrangement of arms, legs, and body in opposing angles, and the serene *Standing Nude* of 1906, a modest adolescent girl in a frontal pose.

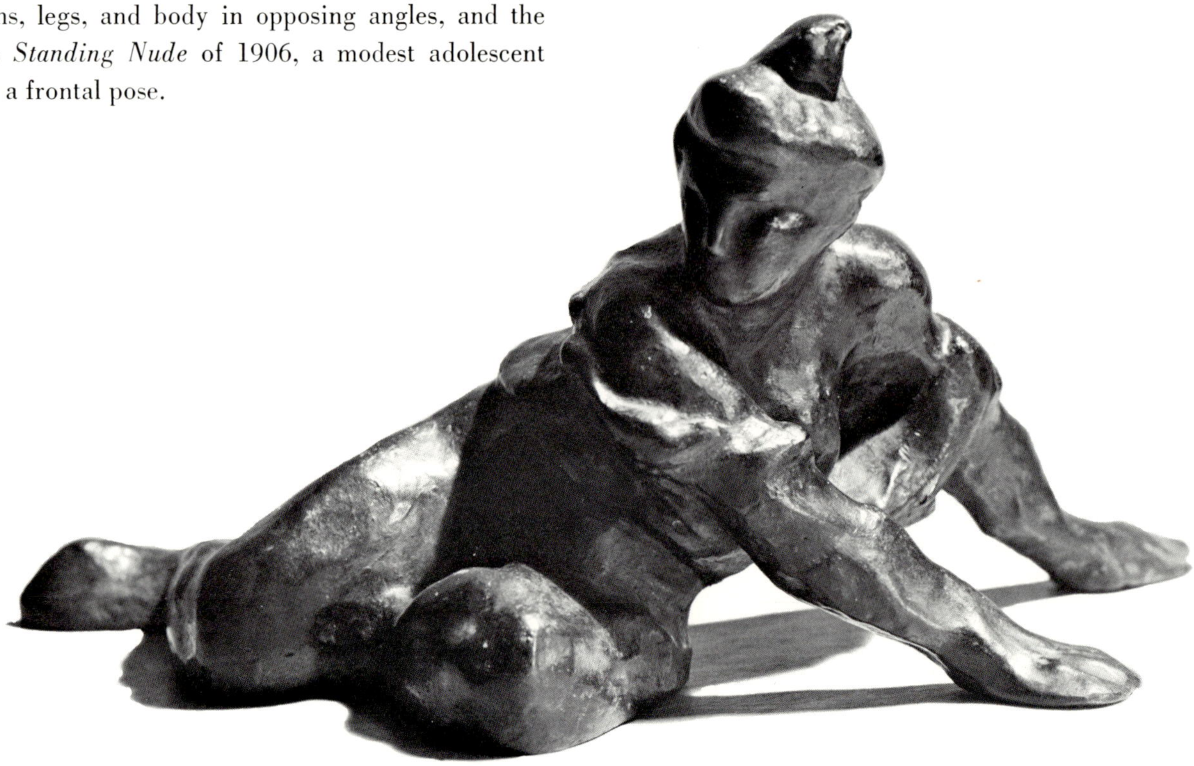

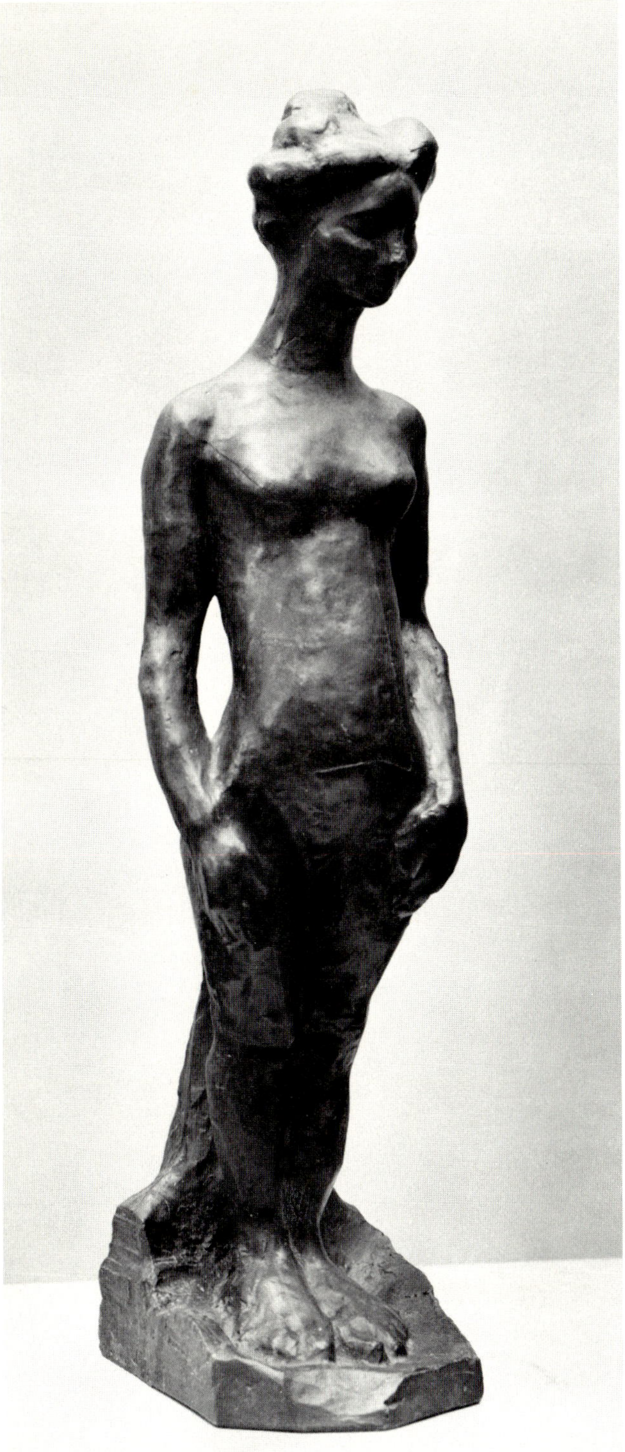

Standing Nude. 1906. 19″ h.

Half-Length Nude, Eyes Cast Down. 1906.
Transfer lithograph

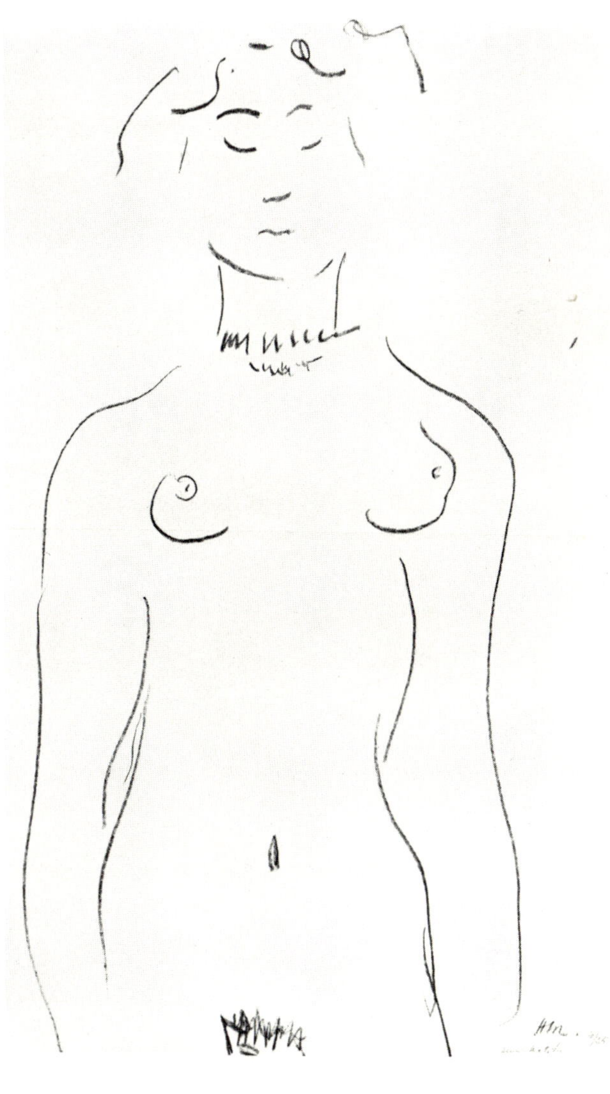

Reclining Woman, II. 1906. Pen and ink

Reclining Figure with Chemise. 1906. $5\frac{1}{2}$" h.

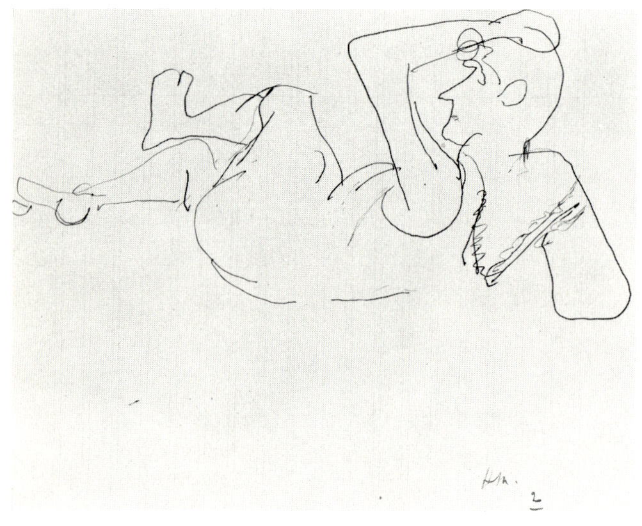

One of the most obsessive recurring themes in Matisse's art is the reclining nude. The earliest sculpture on this theme, which continued to 1929, is *Reclining Figure with Chemise* of 1906, whose pose is closely related to three of the figures in *Joy of Life.* In this bronze, the outstretched figure is supported by the right arm, bent at the elbow; the left knee is thrust over the other leg, twisting the torso and throwing the left hip into dramatic confrontation with the raised left arm. The following year, the theme was more fully developed on a larger scale in *Reclining Nude, I.* While Matisse was working on this figure, it fell and was damaged; before returning to it, the artist made the foremost of his Fauve figure paintings, *Blue Nude (Souvenir of Biskra).* "The bronze," Alfred Barr wrote, "is less imposing in size than *The Blue Nude* yet, in a sense, the big painting actually served as a study for the sculpture. The sculpture is more powerfully composed, the distortions bolder, particularly in the bent but towering left

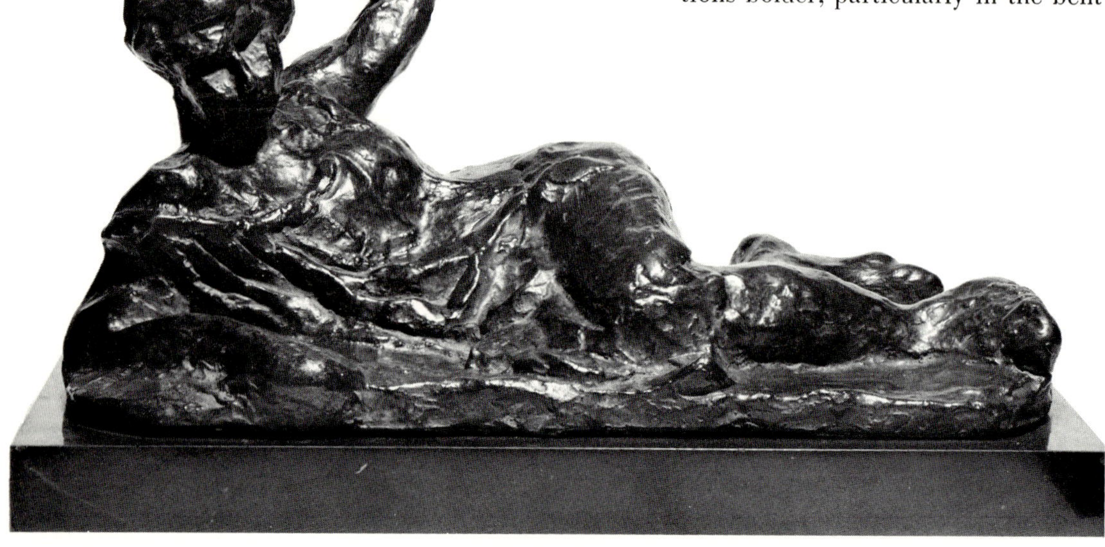

Reclining Nude, I. 1907. 13½" h.

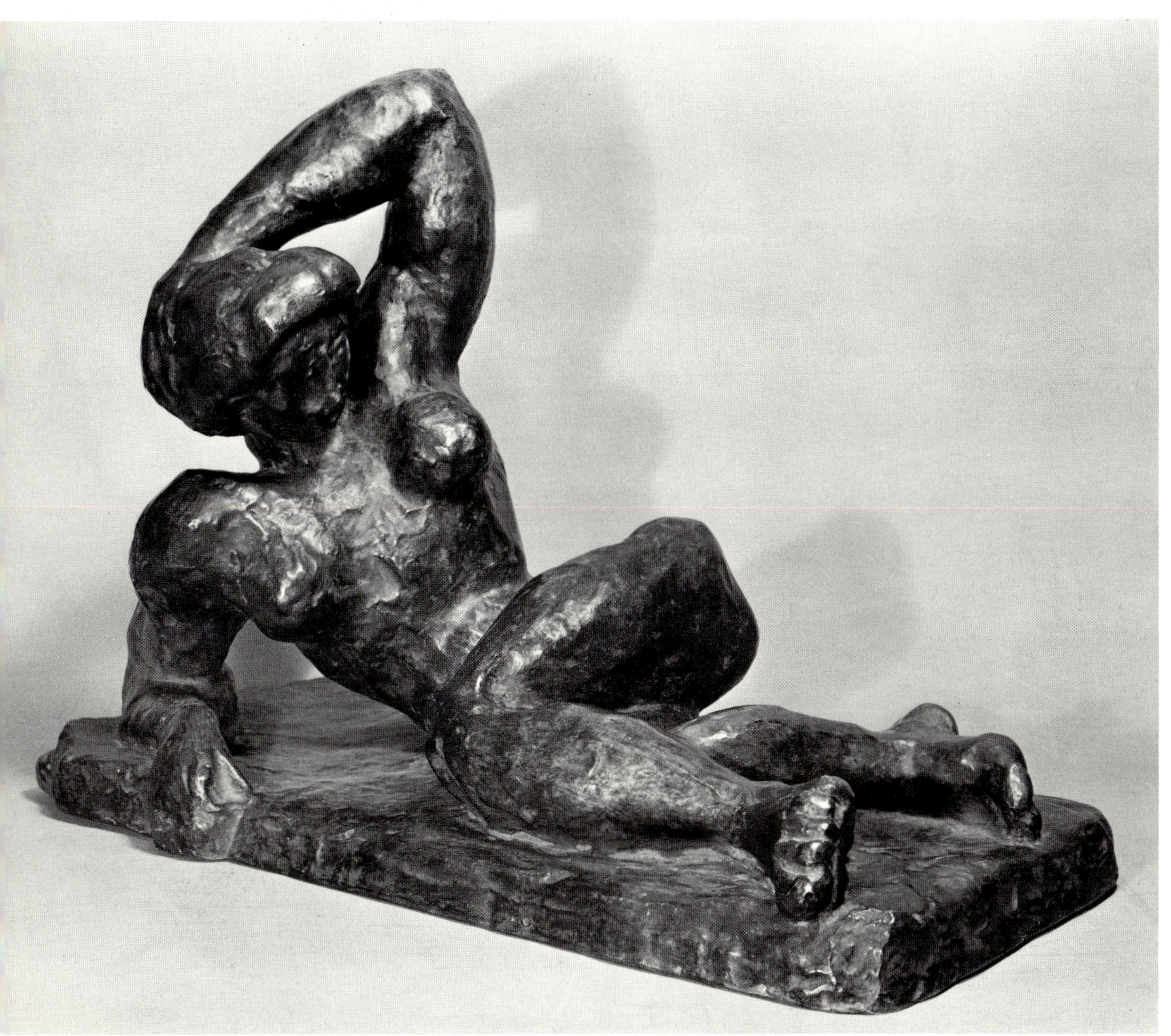

Dance. 1911. 16⅝" h.

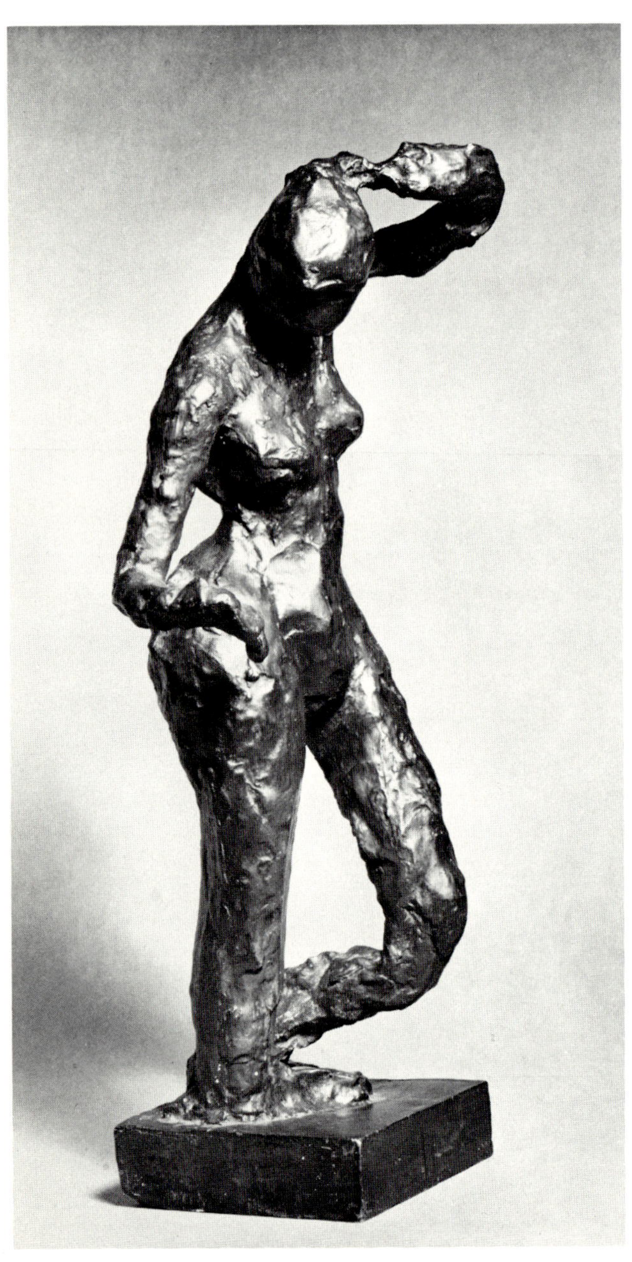

arm. No sculpture by Matisse is more admirably designed to interest the eye and satisfy the sense of rhythmic *contrapposto* when seen from different points of view. *The Reclining Nude* of 1907 is one of Matisse's masterpieces."[6]

In the same year, Matisse produced a unique work in wood called *Dance*.[7] Using a log about six inches in diameter and some seventeen inches long, he carved, in low relief, a frieze of three dancing nudes. This subject absorbed him in the ring dance in *Joy of Life*, and would continue in the two large paintings, *Dance* of 1909 and 1910, as well as in a bronze of 1911.

Matisse's fame was already established in 1908, and his school at 33 Boulevard des Invalides was attracting many foreign students. The curriculum included modeling in clay, and among his remarks, taken down by Sarah Stein (Mrs. Michael Stein), is: "The model must not be made to agree with a preconceived theory or effect. It must impress you, awaken in you an emotion, which in turn you seek to express."[8] Several small crouching nudes created in 1908 range in size from three to seven inches and have in their expressiveness an immediate quality which encourages examination in the hand. *Small Crouching Torso* is headless and armless but is clearly related to the crouching nudes in two paintings of 1907, *Le Luxe, I* and *II*. Three figures seem to be preliminary studies for the larger *Seated Nude (Olga)* of 1910.

Decorative Figure, 1908, combines an archaic dignity with sensuous elegance. The refined and stylized head is large in relation to the body, and as Albert Elsen points out, Matisse ingeniously solved a structural problem with the crossed legs: "Sophisticated

Small Crouching Torso. 1908. $3\frac{1}{8}$" h.

Crouching Nude. 1912. Pen and ink

Small Crouching Nude with Arms. 1908. 6" h.

Small Crouching Nude without an Arm. 1908. $4\frac{3}{4}$" h.

Seated Figure, Right Hand on Ground. 1908. $7\frac{1}{2}$" h.

Seated Nude (Olga). 1910. 17" h.

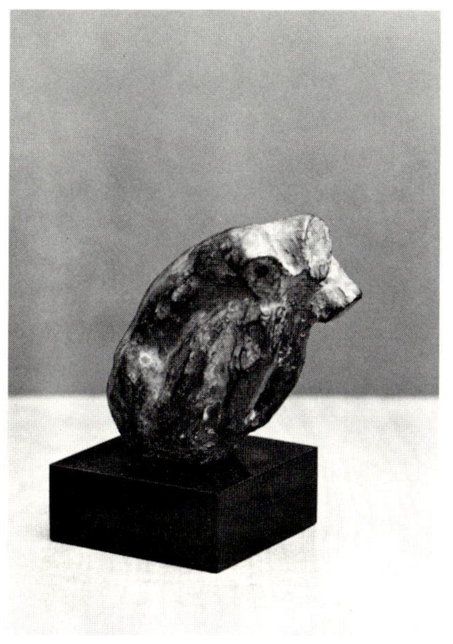

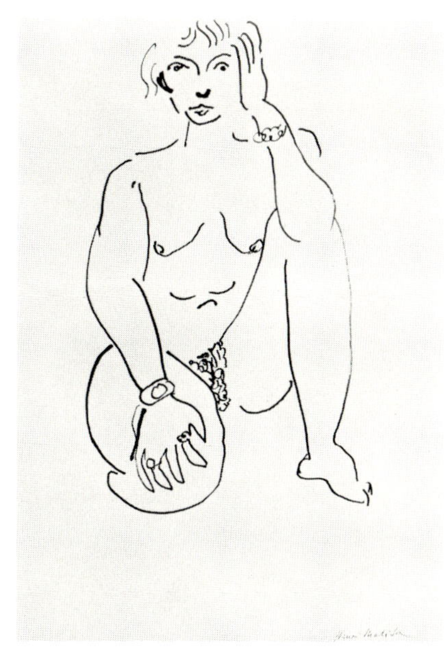

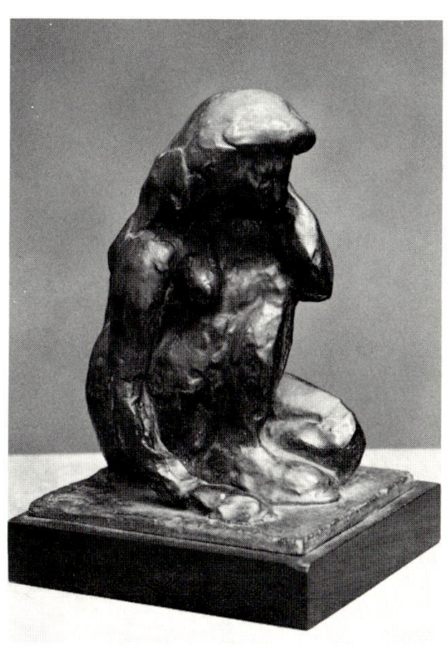

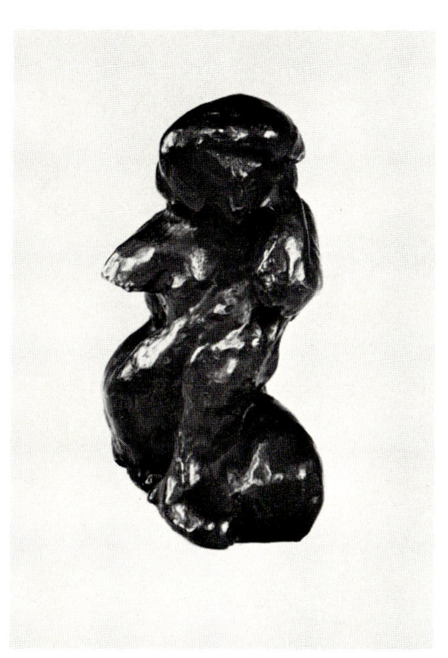

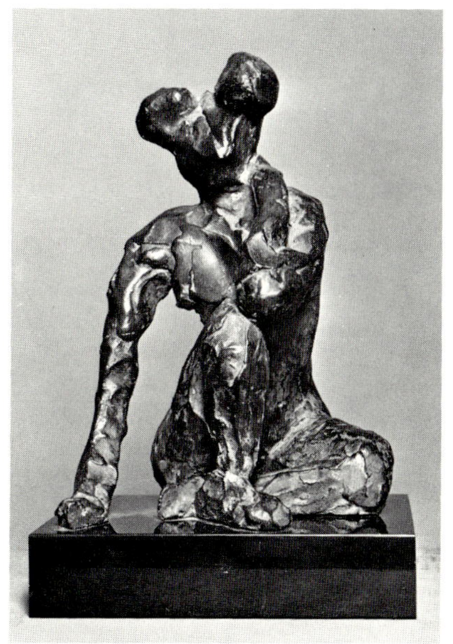

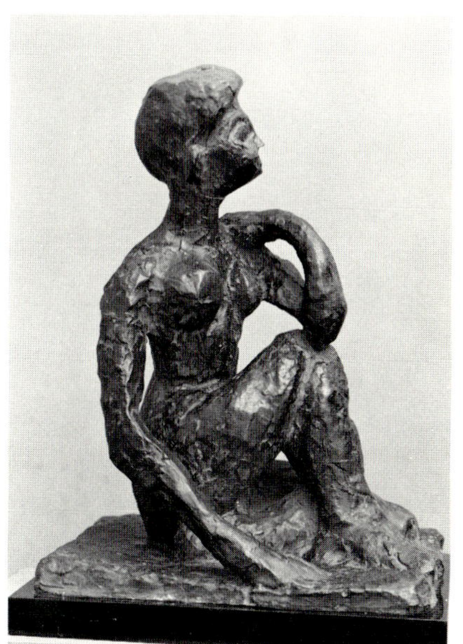

Decorative Figure. 1908. 28¾″ h.

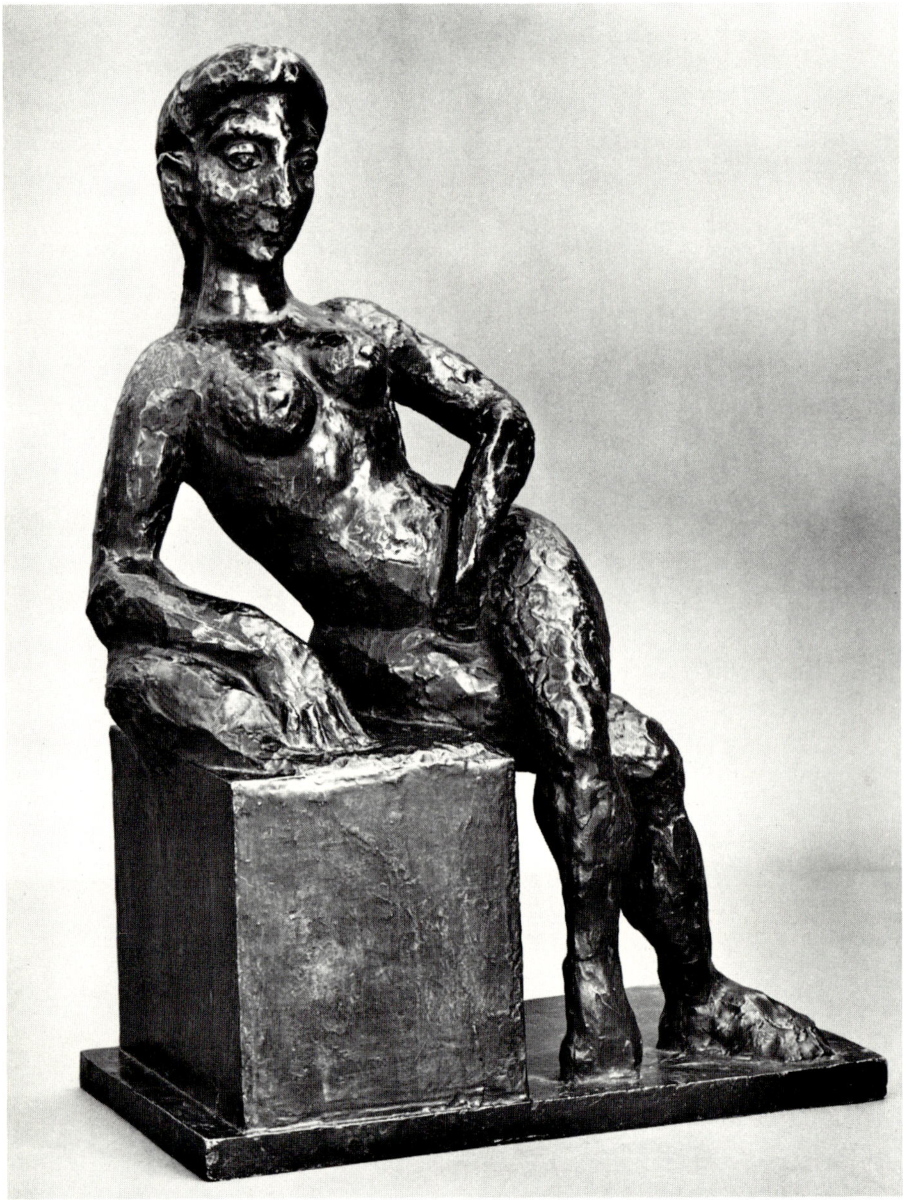

Seated Nude, Arm behind Her Back. 1909. 11⅝″ h.

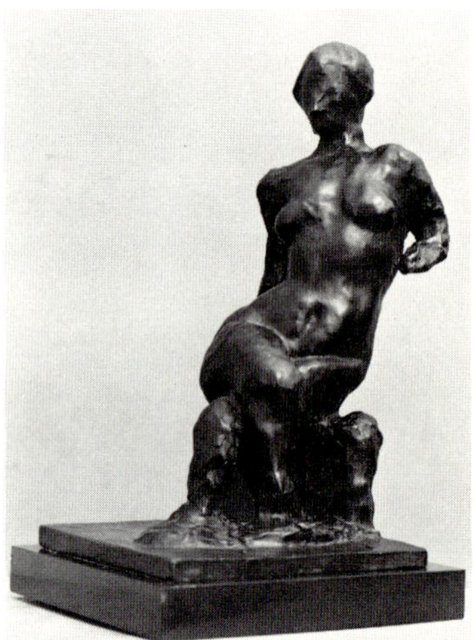

Two Negresses. 1908. 18½" h.

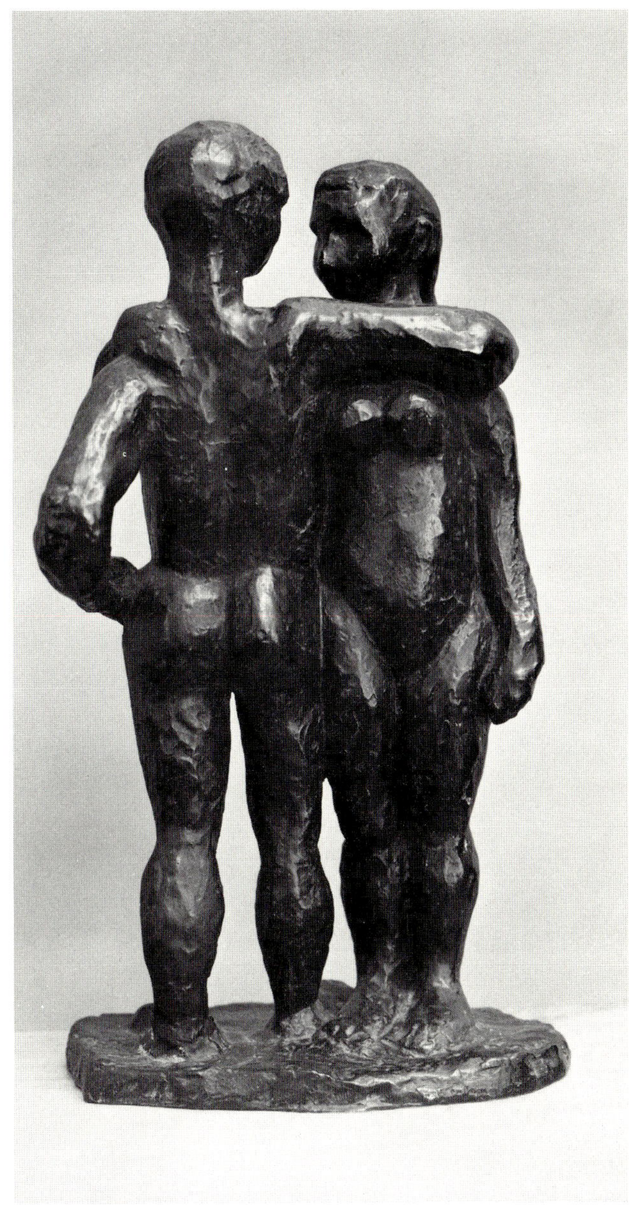

foreshortening of the legs allows both feet to touch the ground (which eliminates a potentially troublesome space below the left foot if it had been kept in the air), and securely anchors the composition."[9] Crossed legs occur again in *Seated Nude, Arm behind Her Back* of 1909. In this piece, the lower legs are left unfinished, and one arm is incomplete, leaving the twisted torso with rounded belly and hip as the focal point.

In *Two Negresses*, 1908, the only sculpture in which Matisse combines two figures, two heavily built nudes stand side to side facing in opposite directions, each with an arm across the other's shoulders. One figure is hermetic, with its left arm hanging close to the body and its legs pressed together; the other, with legs apart and left hand on hip, keeps the composition open.

La Serpentine, 1909, is an elongated figure of a woman with grotesque proportions yet is both dignified and provocative. The nonchalant pose of resting one elbow on a post and crossing the feet at the ankles has been related by Alfred Barr to the Greek tradition.[10] Hilton Kramer has said of this work: "The parts are each given an unexpected weight—the torso as slender as any to be found in a later Giacometti, the head conceived like a flower too large for its stem, the calves almost too absurdly thick for the lean thighs—yet the whole is resolved in a harmony that belies the distortion of the parts."[11]

Standing Nude, a small bas-relief of 1908, seems like a sketch in bronze for *The Back, I*, 1909, the first of four in the great series of more than life-size reliefs. Although the small relief is a frontal view, its fluent modeling is an exercise in highlighting form which was

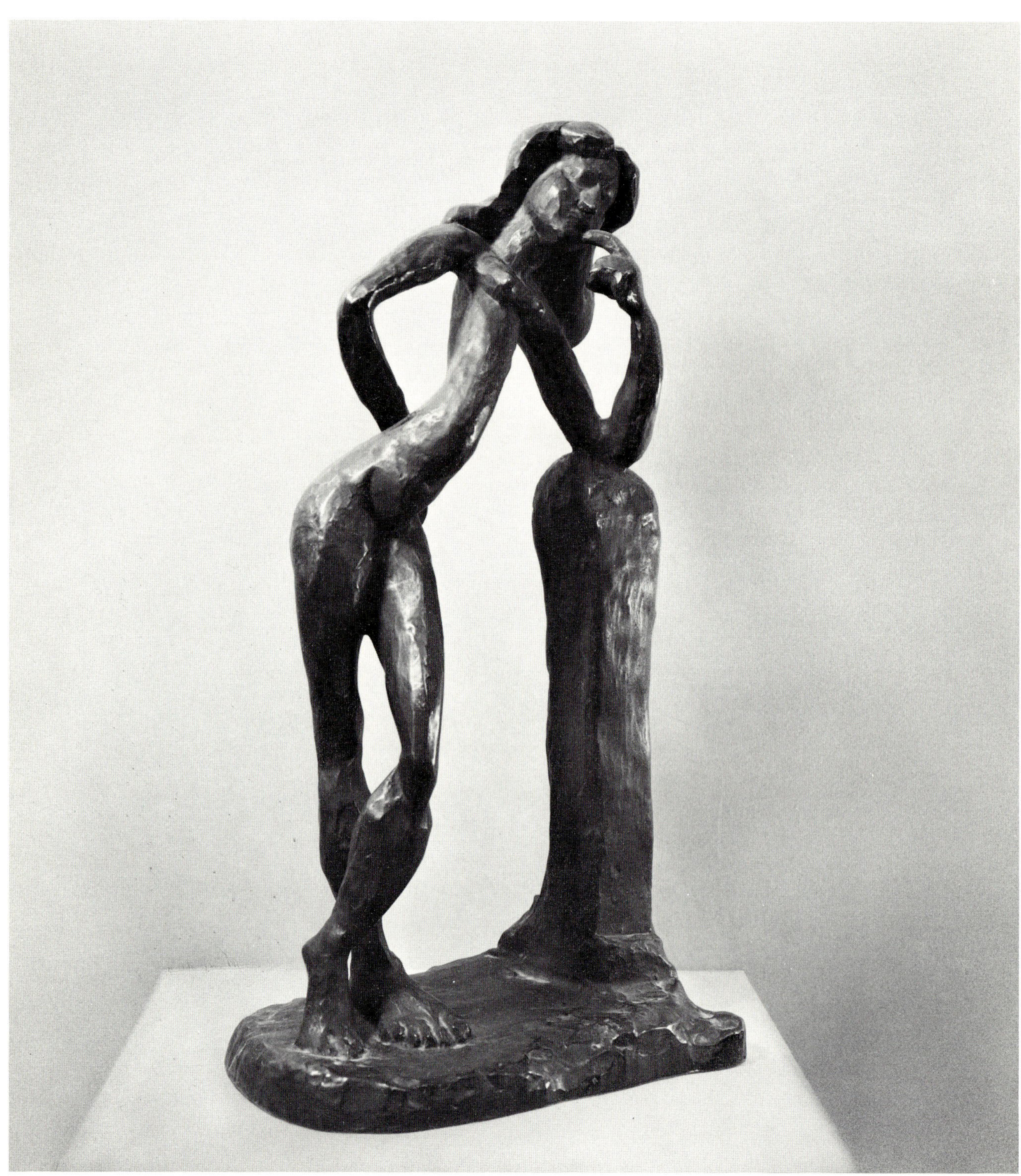

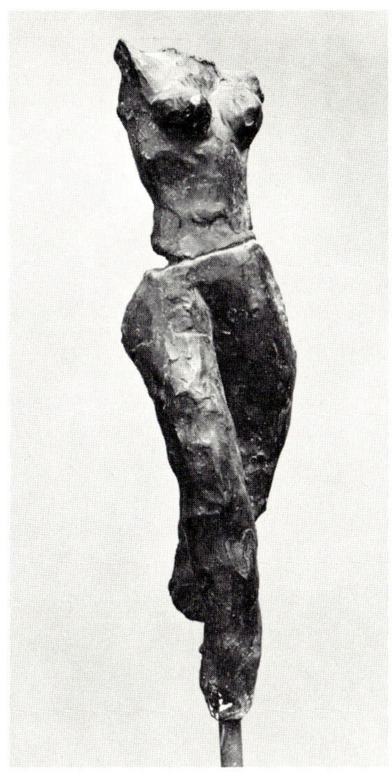

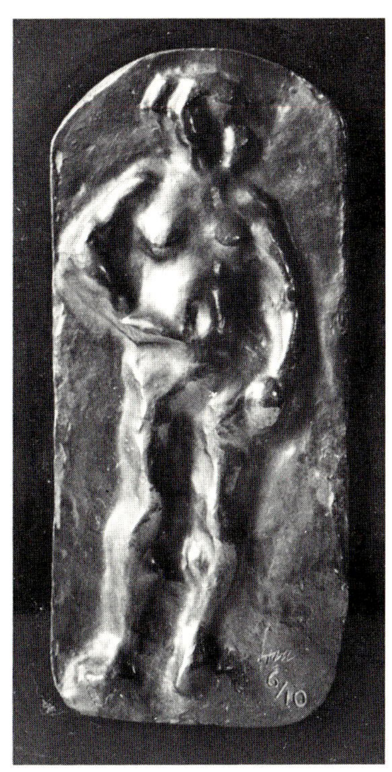

FACING PAGE: *La Serpentine*. 1909. 22¼″ h.

Torso without Arms or Head. 1909. 9¾″ h.

Standing Nude. 1908. 9″ h.

carried to the Back series in a successively abstract manner until the fourth and final version of 1930.

Because of the need for space to work on a commission from the Russian collector, Sergei I. Shchukin, for two large wall decorations *(Dance* and *Music)*, Matisse moved to Issy-les-Moulineaux where he built a studio. Perhaps the experience of working out the problems of form in murals led him to attempt a large relief. The naturalistic modeling in *The Back, I* accentuates the form of the heavy-set model, who leans to the left with her head beyond the academic point of balance—above the weight-bearing foot. The curving arabesque (a characteristic of Matisse's that was already apparent in sculptures such as *Reclining Nude, I*, 1907, and *Decorative Figure*, 1908) flows from the head, cradled in the left elbow, down the furrow of the spine and rounded buttock to the bent right knee. As if to suggest a figure in the round, a full breast is shown, where in actuality it would not be visible. In another distortion, the fingers of the twisted right hand are spread out as a fan against the wall.

The Back, II was done in 1913 and, like the first version, the figure is placed off center. The stance, however, is more stabilized. The flowing rhythm changes to a syncopated one, and the modeling has Cubist facets and arbitrary creases, such as at the waist and buttocks; counter movements occur in the rounded right shoulder and curved left arm. Hair and neck become a single shaft extending into the hollow of the back, foretelling the process of simplification to come in the later states.

In 1916–17 Matisse was working on the large painting *Bathers by a River*, in which details of one figure appear in *The Back, III*, 1916–17. In this relief, the

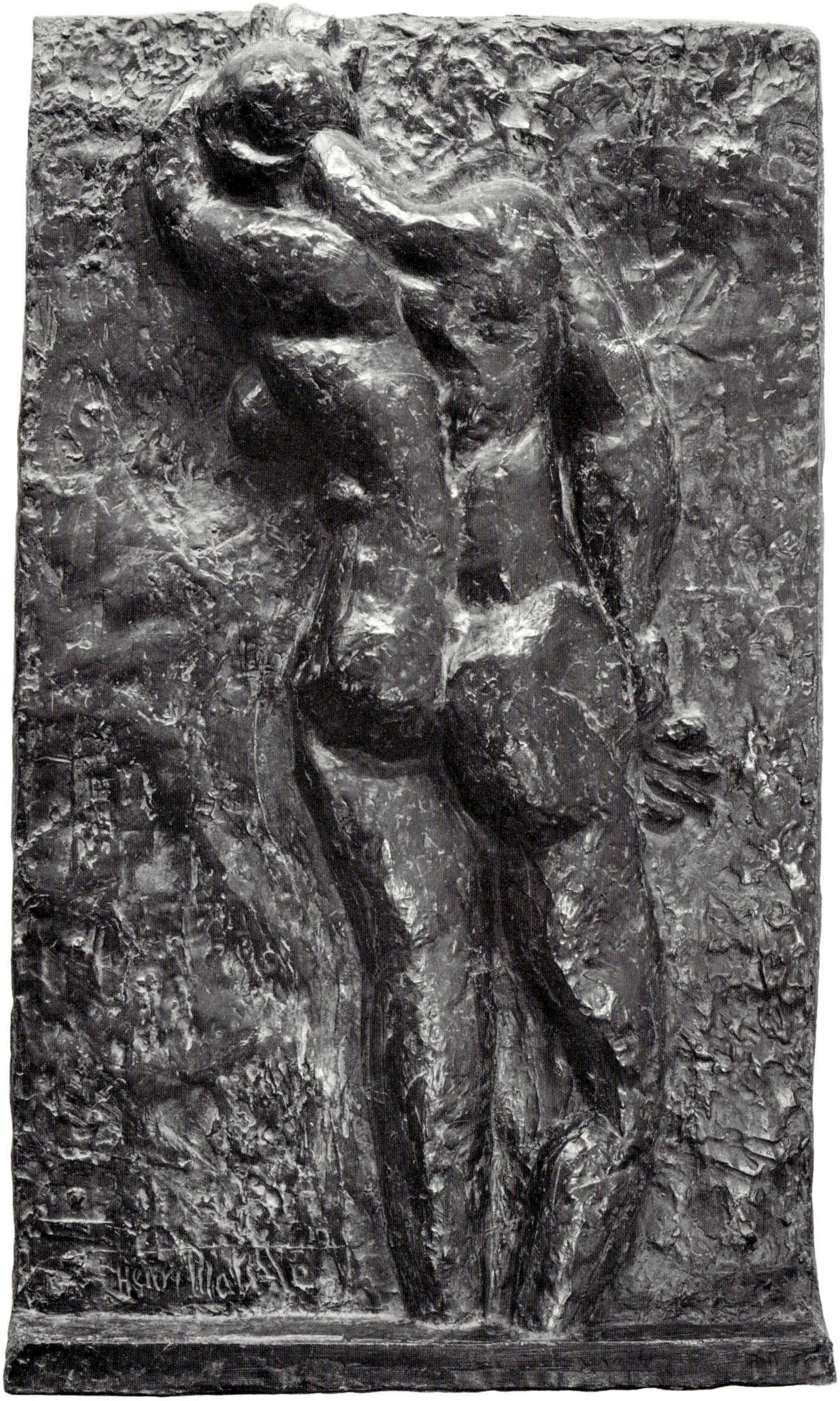

The Back, I. 1909. 74⅜″ h.

Study for *The Back, II.* ca. 1913. Pen and ink

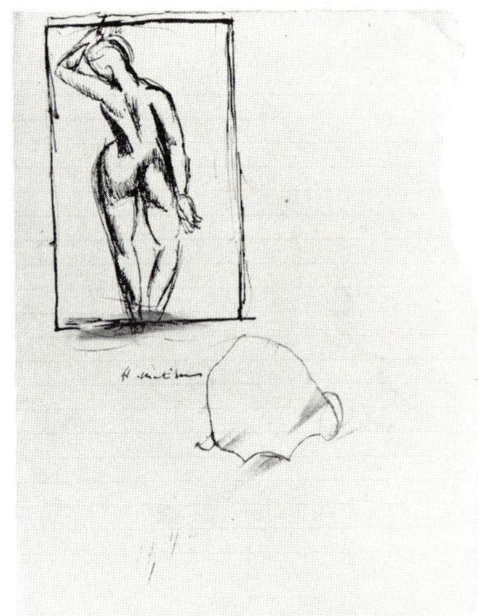

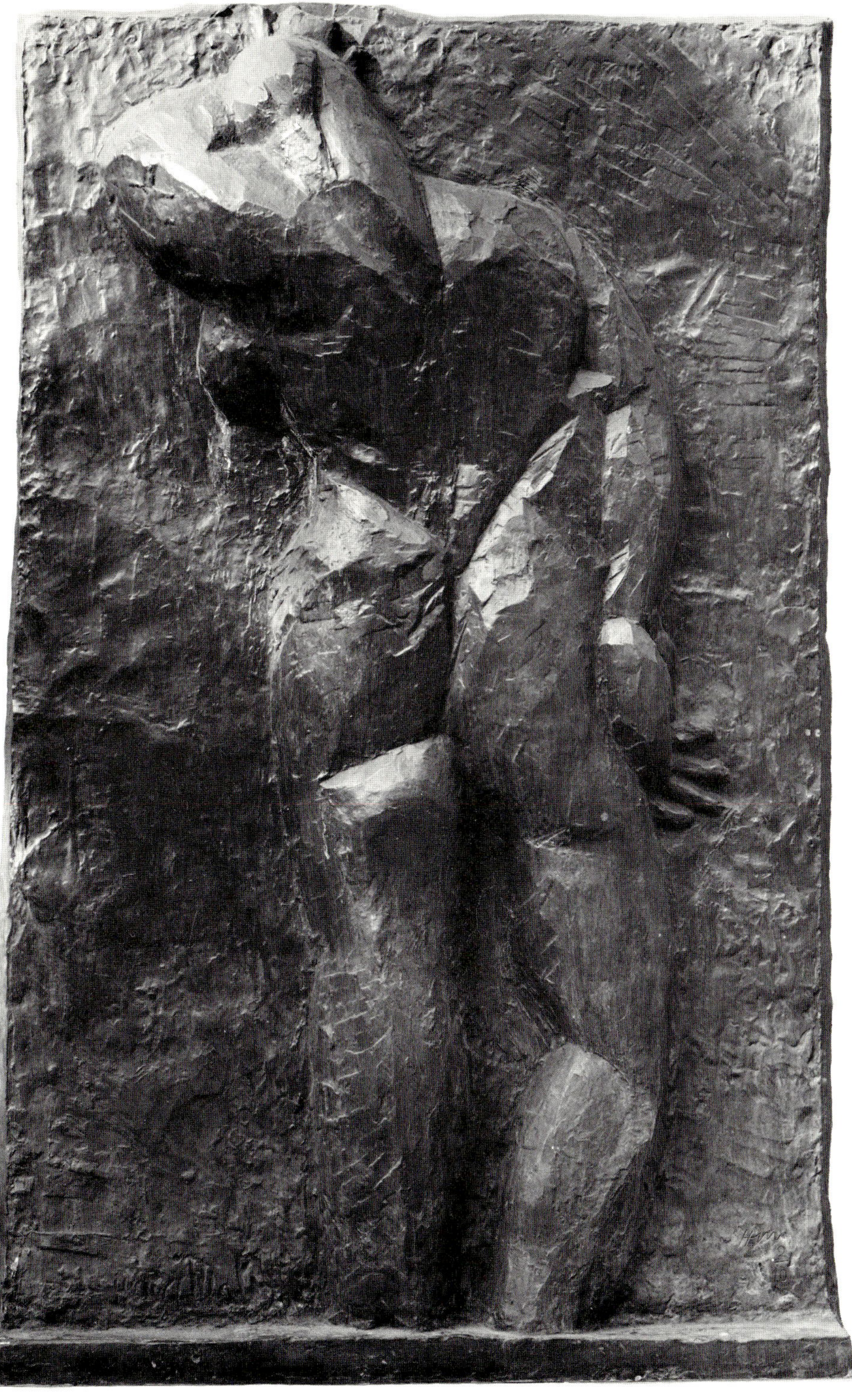

The Back, II. 1913. 74½" h.

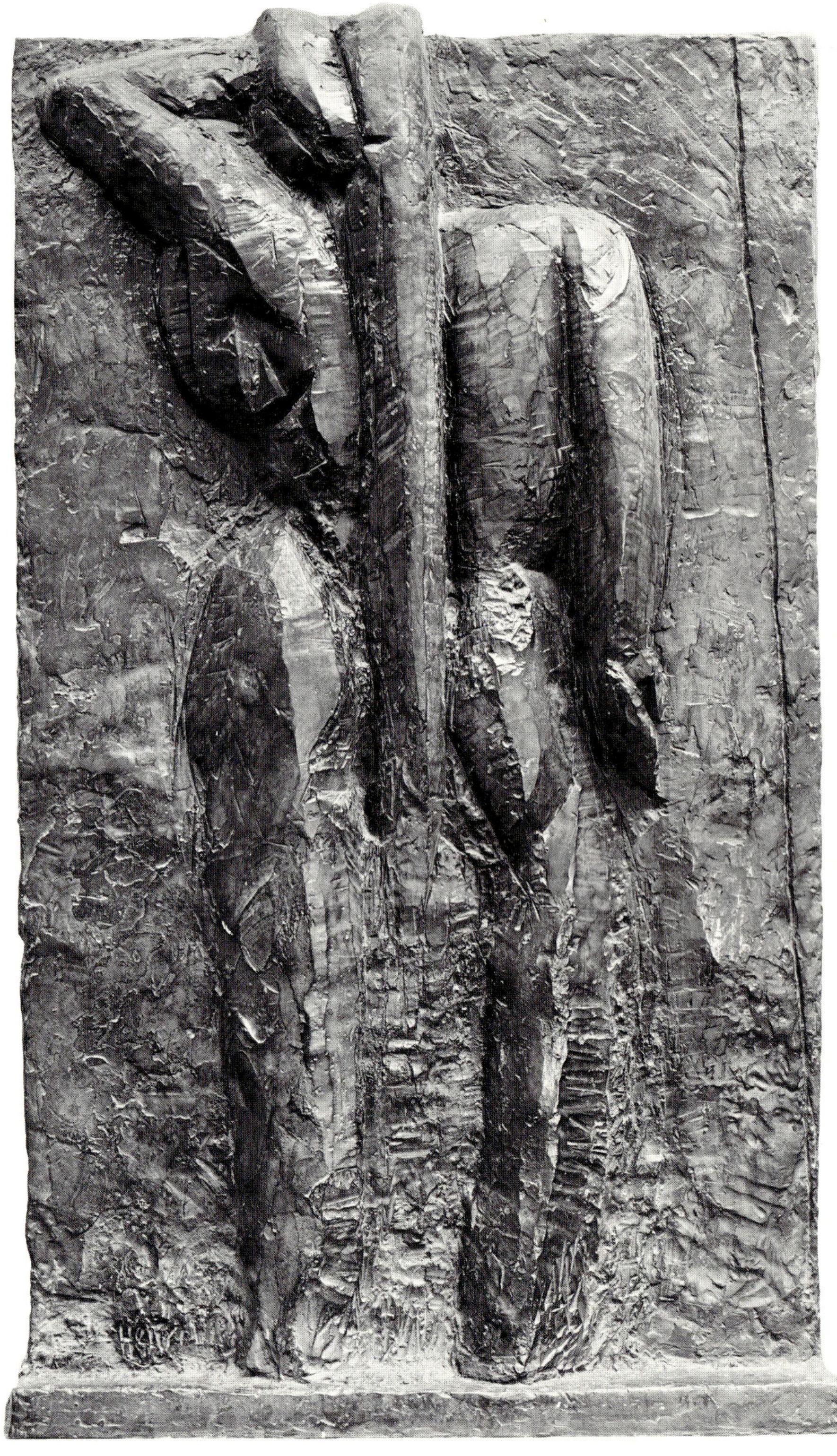

The Back, III. 1916–17. 74½″ h.

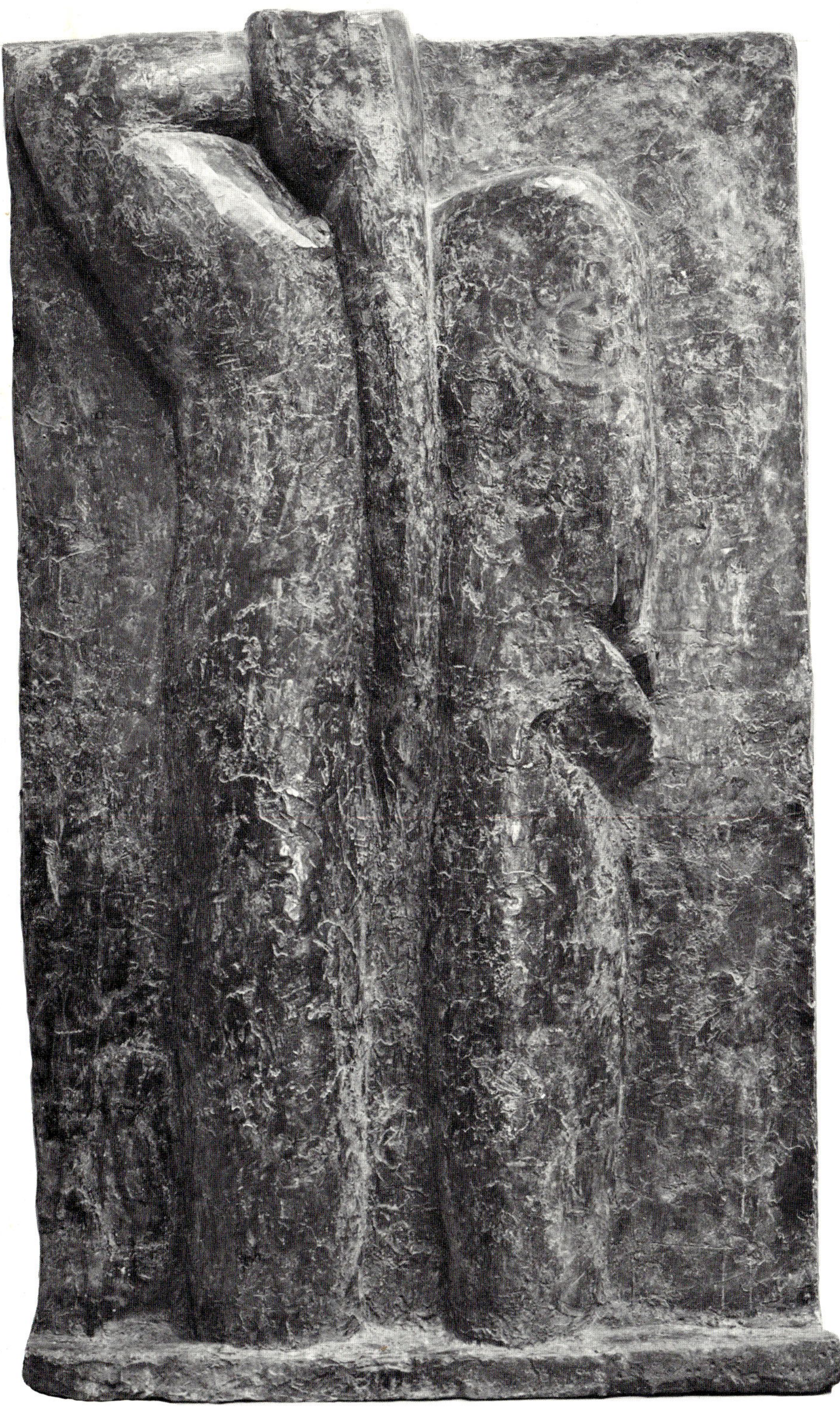

The Back, IV. 1930. 74½" h.

Jeannette, I. 1910–13. 13″ h.

Jeannette, II, 1910–13. 10⅜″ h.

Jeannette, III. 1910–13. 23¾″ h.

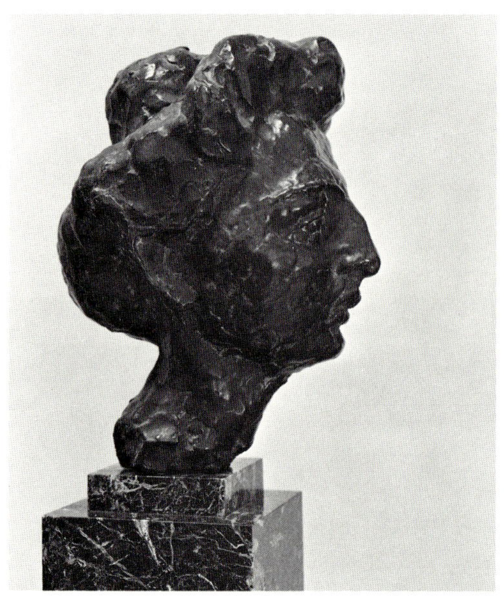

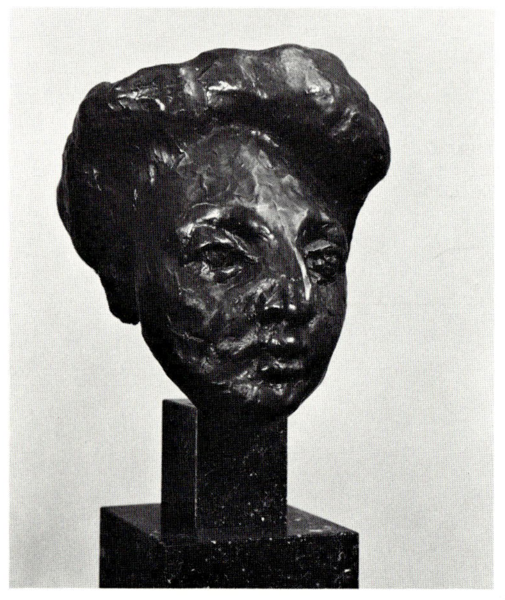

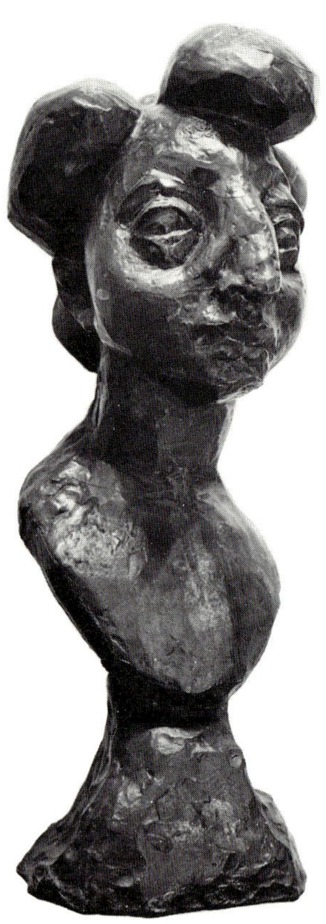

torso is squared off, with the long hair dividing the form into four main masses. The hips and legs are fused, with only a vestige of anatomical form, and the splayed fingers are eliminated.

Matisse worked on *The Back, IV* in Nice in 1929–30. In this, as in the third version, the figure is centered, and the left breast is no longer visible. The top of the head protrudes above the edge of the panel, breaking the conventional format of the bas-relief as picture plane, and introducing an architectural device of combining the figure with its support. In the final resolution

Jeannette, IV. 1910–13. 24⅛" h.

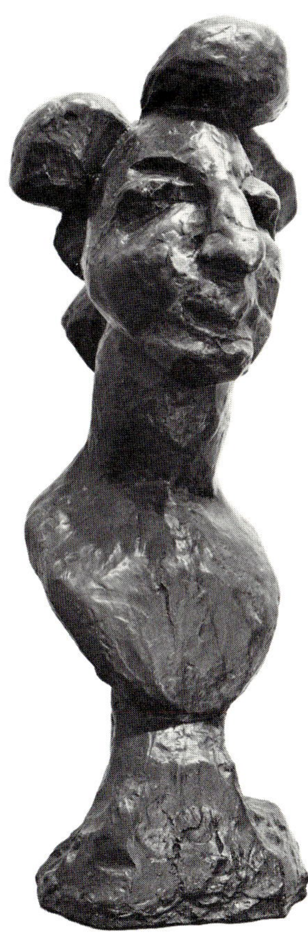

Jeannette, V. 1910–13. 22⅞" h.

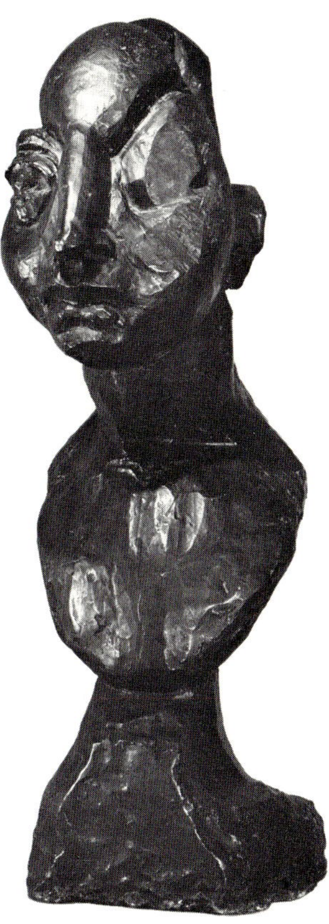

of the bent left arm, the point of the elbow appears to be the actual corner of the relief. The heavy rope of hair becomes the division of two columns, the right one notched to indicate the hand. The long evolution of these great sculptures can explain the radical change between the first and the last, but what is also apparent is that Matisse was taking logical but ever bolder steps toward monumental sculpture.

In another important series, the five heads of Jeannette of 1910–13, Matisse radically altered his originally naturalistic conception. In 1910 he worked on the first two versions directly from the model, a young woman named Jeanne Vaderin. Within three years, the remaining heads were produced as variations, intensifying the pear-shaped face, aquiline features, and bouffant hair in the third and fourth versions, and drastically simplifying the structure in the fifth. Here, working from the plaster cast of the third version, Matisse lopped off the center roll of hair, building up the brow instead, and sliced off the sides of the head, throwing the eye sockets into relief. The final step was to fill in the left socket with an abstract block, giving

Head of Marguerite. 1915. 12⅝" h.

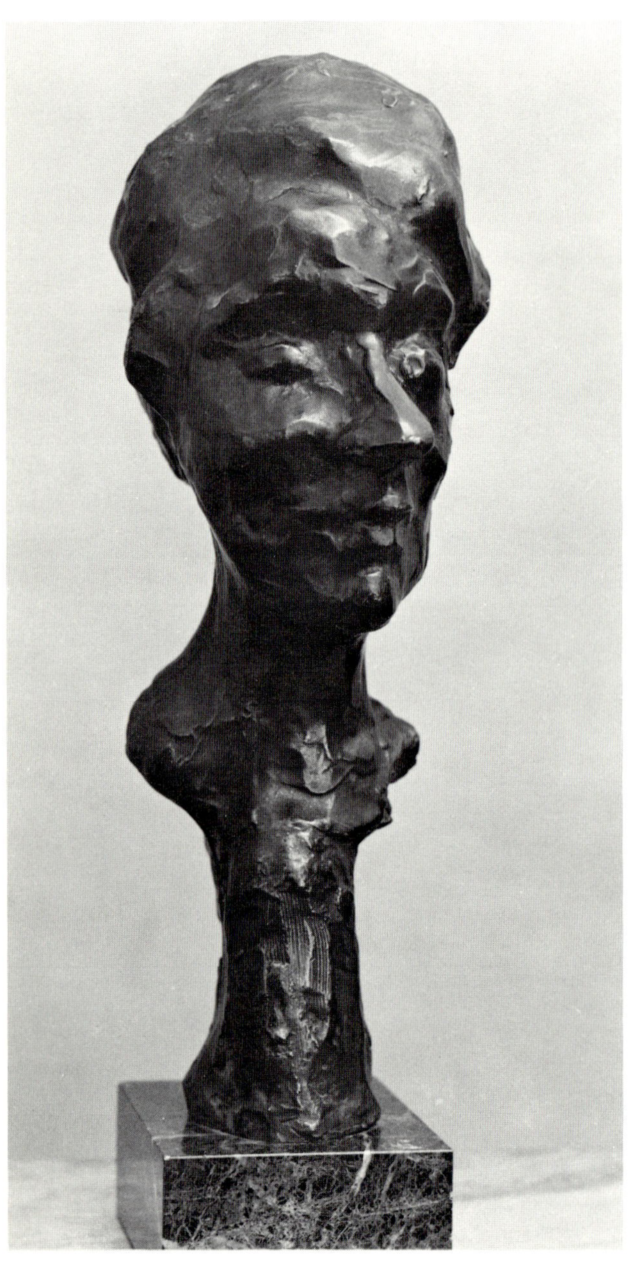

an ambiguous intensity to the face. Alfred Barr has said that *Jeannette, V* is bolder than any Cubist sculpture of the period, and that it anticipates Picasso's big plaster heads of 1932.[12] While the process of abstraction in these heads is clearly evident, Matisse also demonstrates his extraordinary mastery of organic form and its expressive possibilities.

In 1915 Matisse modeled an eloquent head of his daughter; in *Head of Marguerite* a thin face is supported by a narrow bust that turns into a truncated stele, which has caused it often to be called "Giacomettesque," although, of course, it antedates Giacometti's attenuated pieces by thirty years.

In 1916 Matisse began to spend winters in Nice. Of the three small bronzes of 1918, two were probably taken from Hellenistic sources, and *Reclining Nude with Bolster* relates to paintings of this period, when he was embarking on another major theme—the odalisque. In 1921 he moved into an apartment and was to spend a good part of every year in Nice, whose Mediterranean sun and light are captured in hundreds of paintings in which he combined patterned textiles, exotic plants, and models, both nude and gaily costumed.

George Besson wrote of Matisse's life in Nice that he would visit the School of Decorative Arts to study a cast of Michelangelo's *Night,* one of the pair made for the Medici tomb in Florence.[13] During 1923–25, a sculpture evolved which combines the indolence of the painted odalisques with an extraordinary vitality and tension. The massive torso of *Large Seated Nude,* leaning sharply backward with the arms locked behind the head, is like an architectural cantilever anchored by the left foot under the right knee. The fact that the thighs

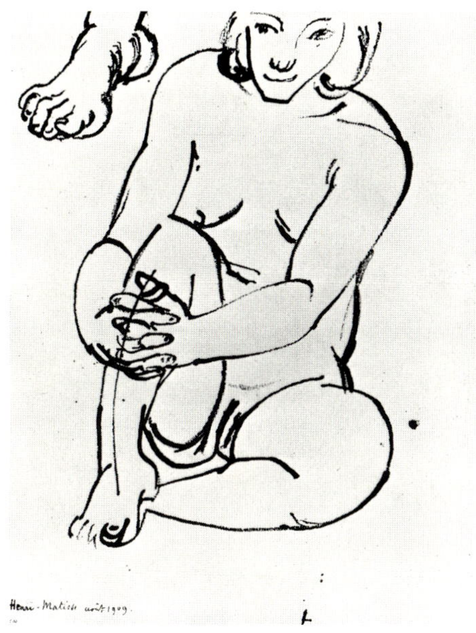

Seated Model Clasping Knee. 1909. Reed pen and ink

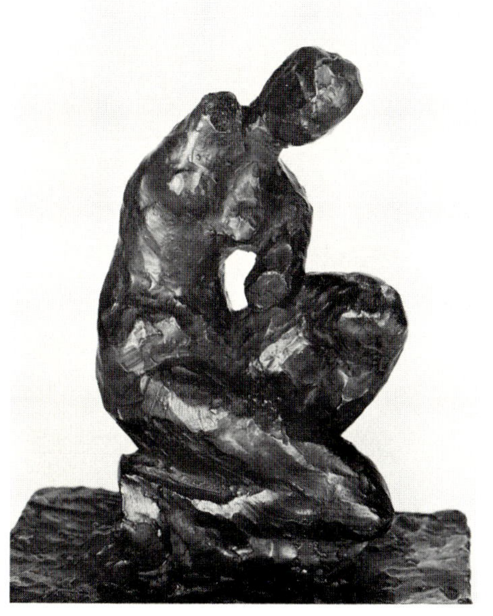

Venus. ca. 1918. $10\frac{1}{4}''$ h.

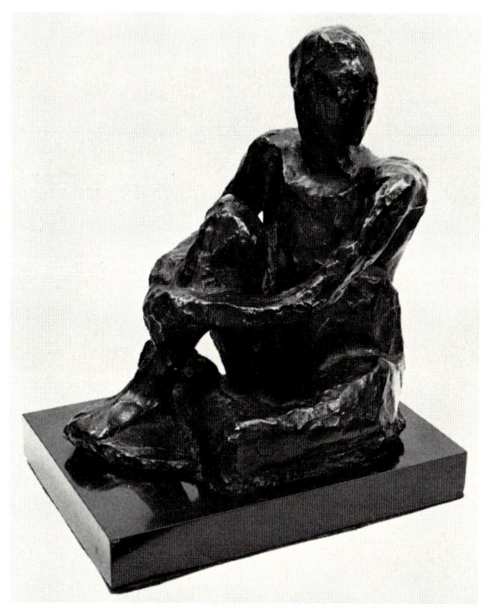

Seated Nude Clasping Her Right Leg. 1918. 9″ h.

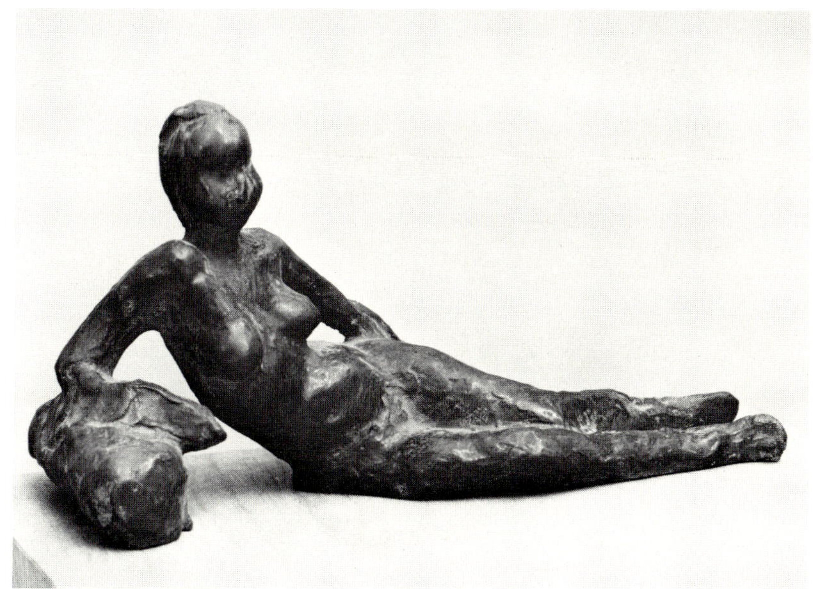

Reclining Nude with Bolster. 1918. $4\frac{3}{4}''$ h.

Large Seated Nude. 1923–25. 33″ h.

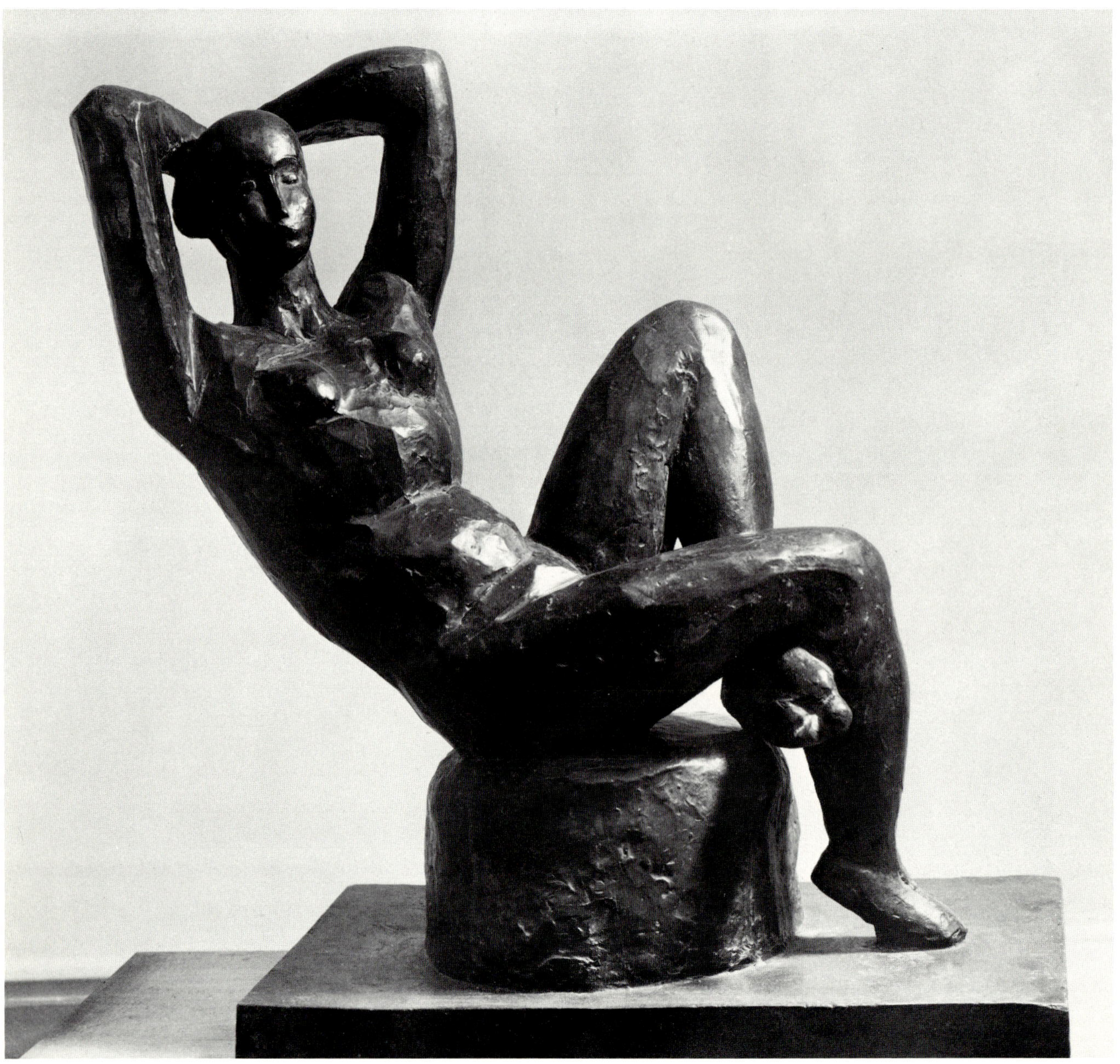

Day. 1922. Lithograph

Small Nude in an Armchair. 1924. 9½″ h.

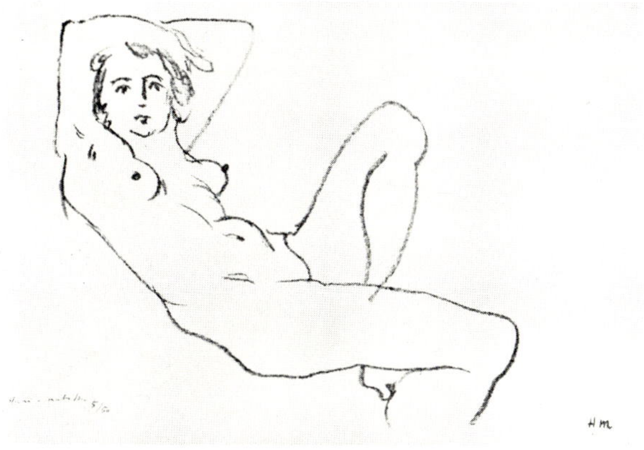

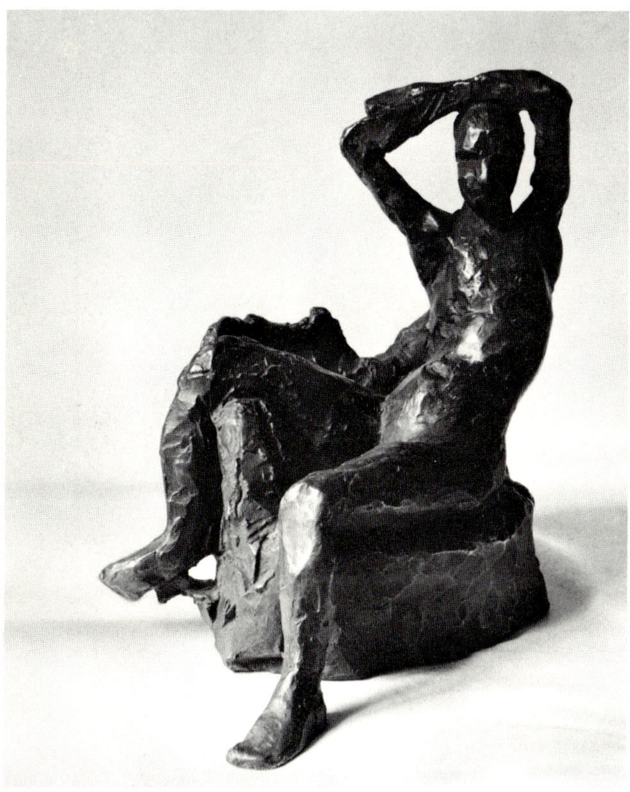

and legs are unusually short compared with the torso is one of the most fascinating things about this sculpture. Perhaps their fleshy bulk is all that is needed to support the leaning body. In a small bronze of 1924, the nude, in a similar position in a low armchair, nonchalantly throws one leg over the back of the chair.

In a series of three heads of 1925–29, the transformation from naturalism occurs in three steps, done at two-year intervals. The first, of 1925, is a conventional portrait of the model, Henriette Darricarrère, who posed for many paintings and drawings in Nice during the 1920s. *Henriette, II*, 1927, introduces a style of simplified planes and volumes that Matisse was to use occasionally in future sculptures. It is in *Henriette III*, though, that the personality of the model is revealed. The lines of the jaw are sharpened and the high cheek bones emphasized; the facial muscles around the mouth are tightened, leaving it partly open as if to speak. While these sculptures are only slightly over life size, one can imagine them in monumental scale, especially the third version, with its architectural base.

In 1927 and 1929, Matisse returned to the pose of the reclining nudes of 1906–07. In *Reclining Nude, II* he reverses the position, with the head at the right and the torso extending to the left. The body is less contorted than in the 1907 version, and the figure, propped up by the left elbow with the right one in the air, is monumental in its passivity, emphasizing the swell of the rounded buttocks. In *Reclining Nude, III*, the rugged modeling yields to the smooth, and the sinuous body has a relaxed ease.

Continuing in this manner of organic simplicity, Matisse produced two very small torsos in 1929 and the

Henriette, I. 1925. $11\frac{1}{2}$" h.

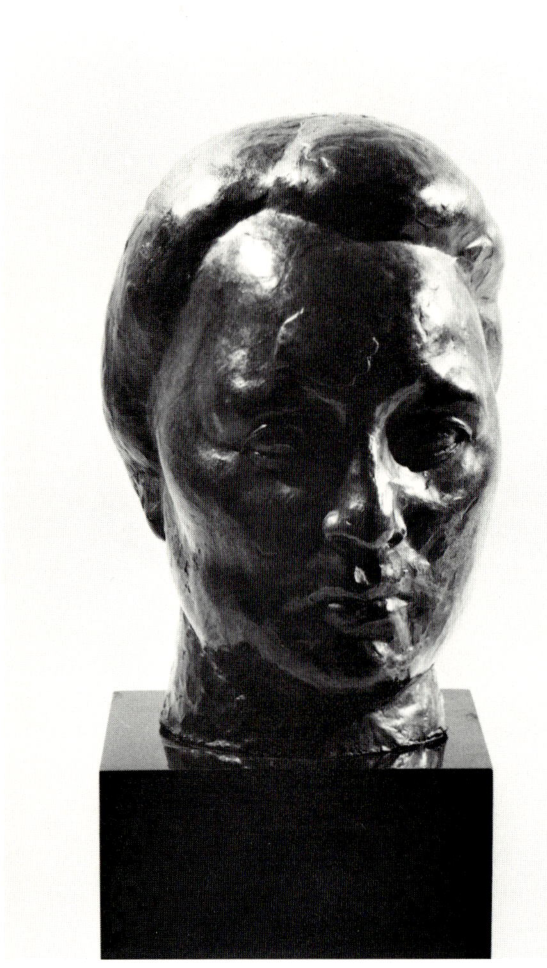

Henriette, II. 1927. $12\frac{5}{8}$" h.

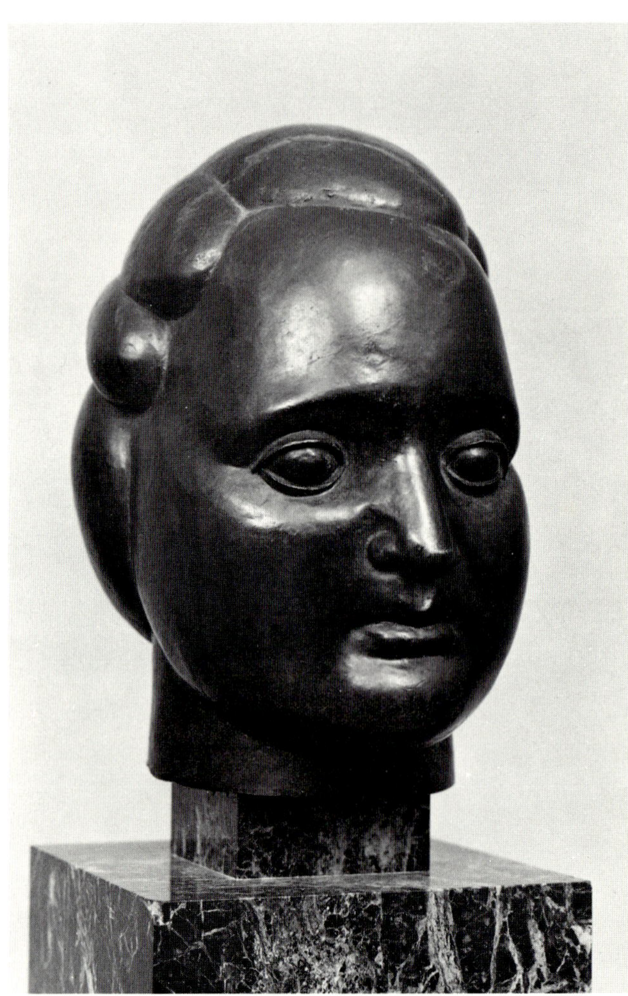

Henriette, III. 1929. 15¾" h.

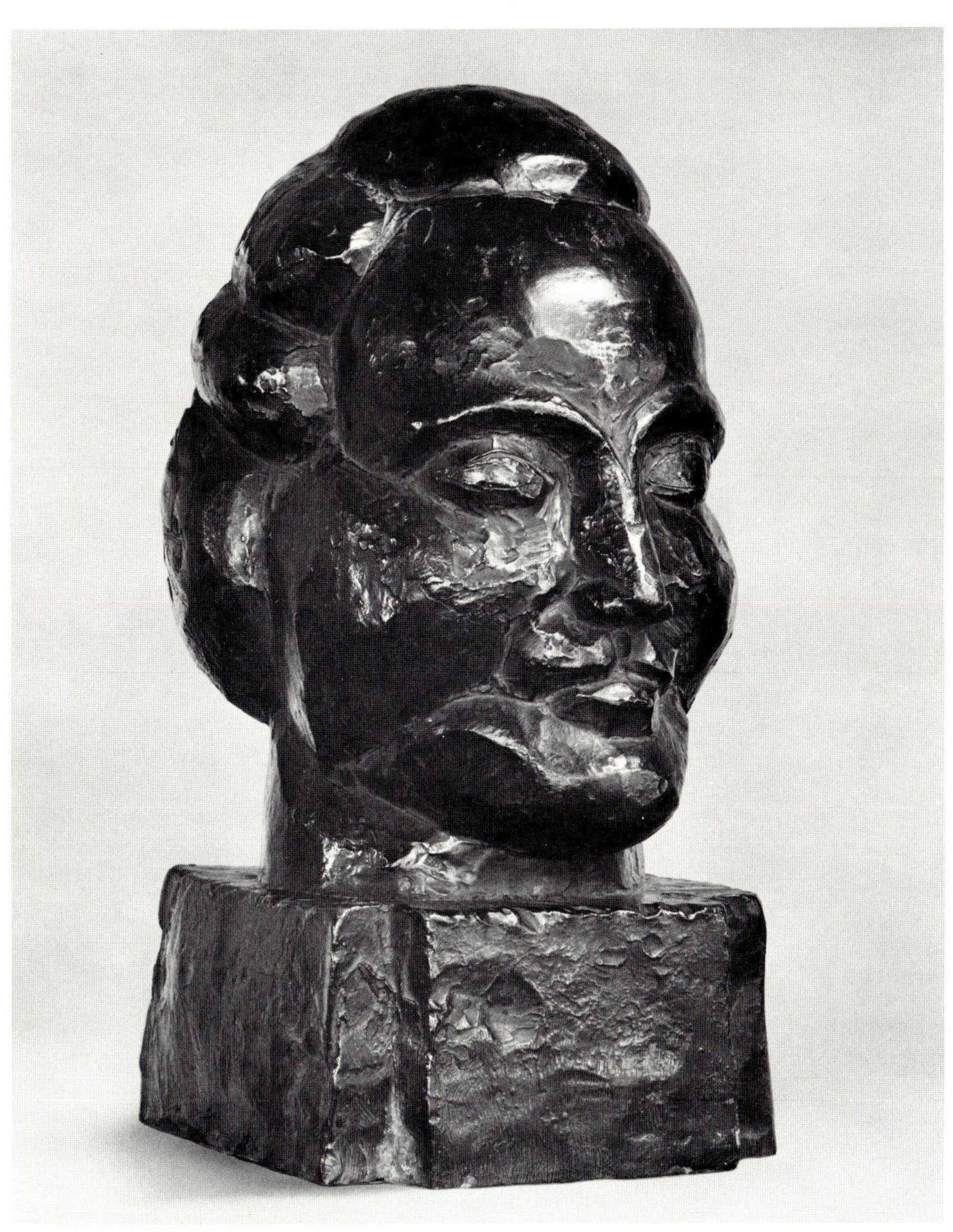

Reclining Nude, II. 1927. 11½" h.

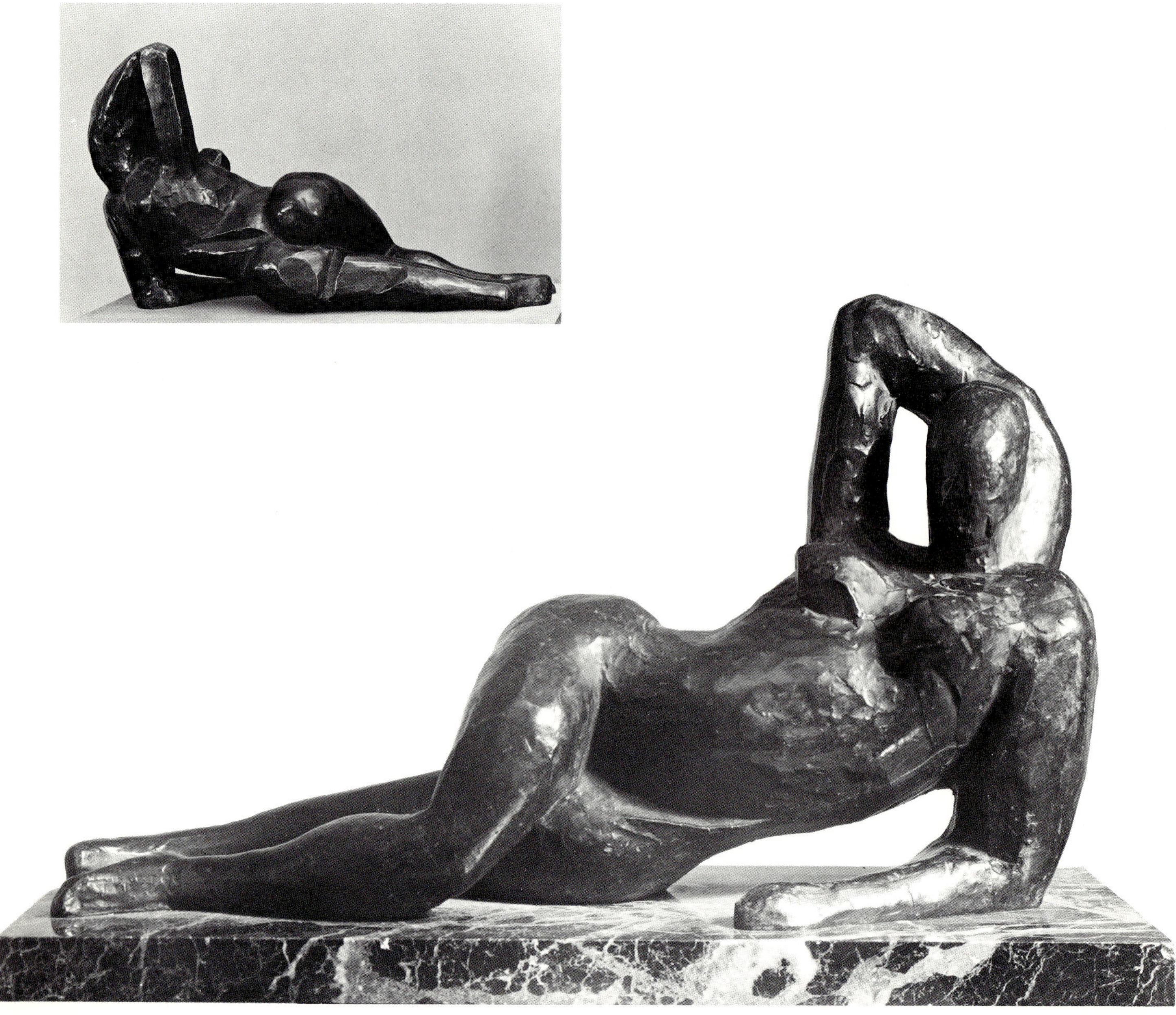

Reclining Nude, III. 1929. 7¼" h.

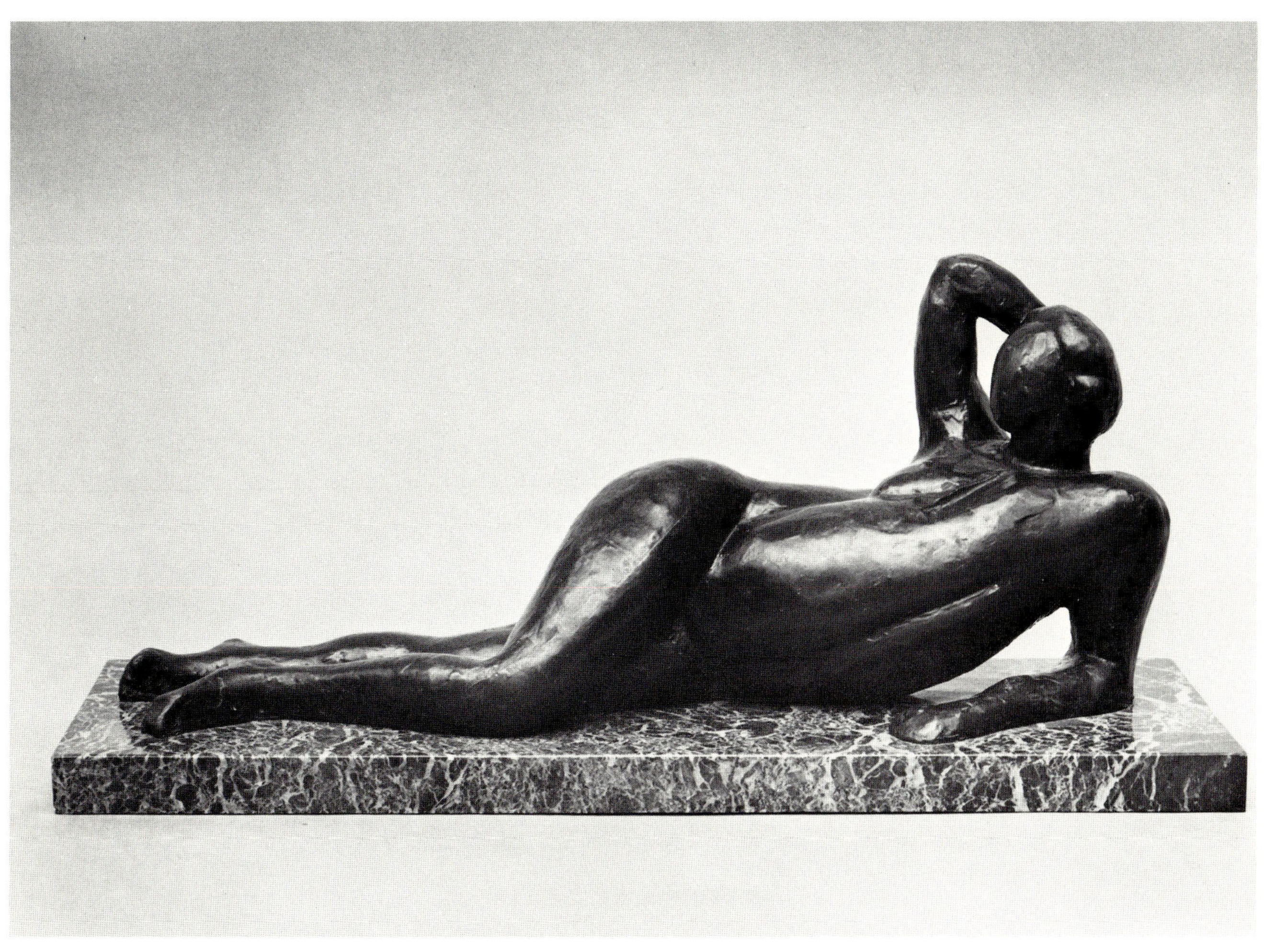

Small Thin Torso.
1929. 3″ h.

Small Torso. 1929. 3½″ h.

Tiari. 1930. 8″ h.

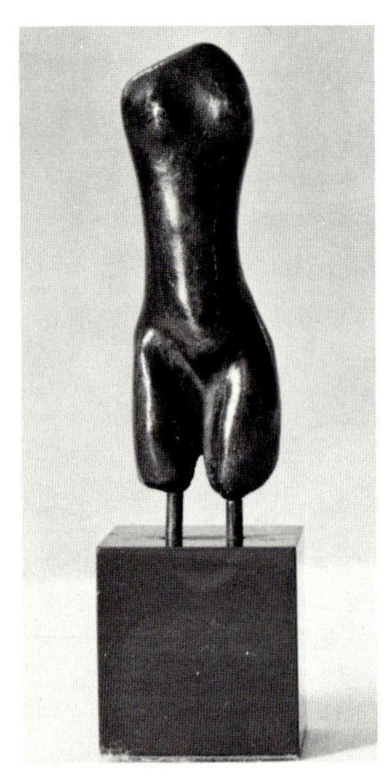

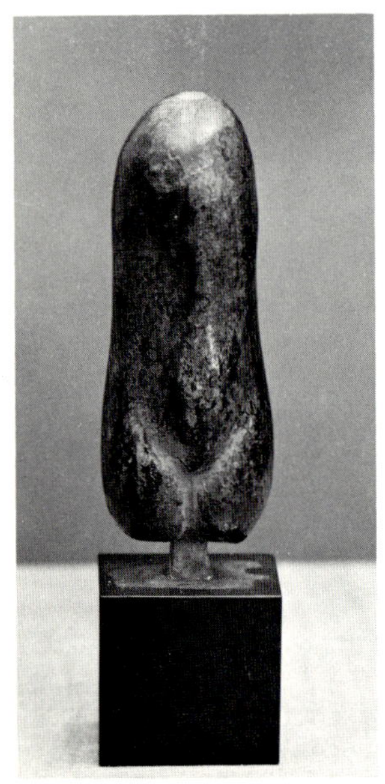

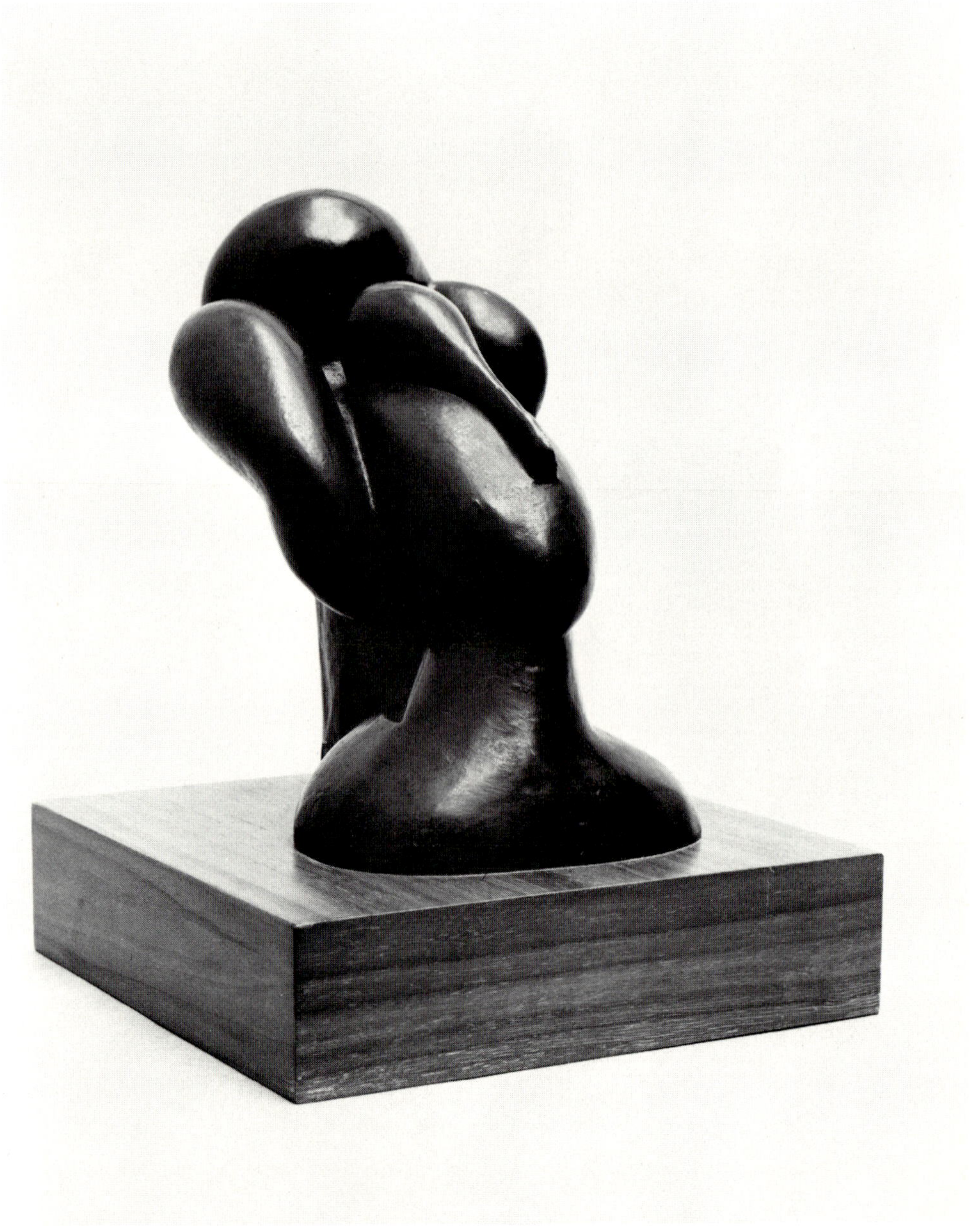

Tiari (with Necklace). 1930. 8″ h.

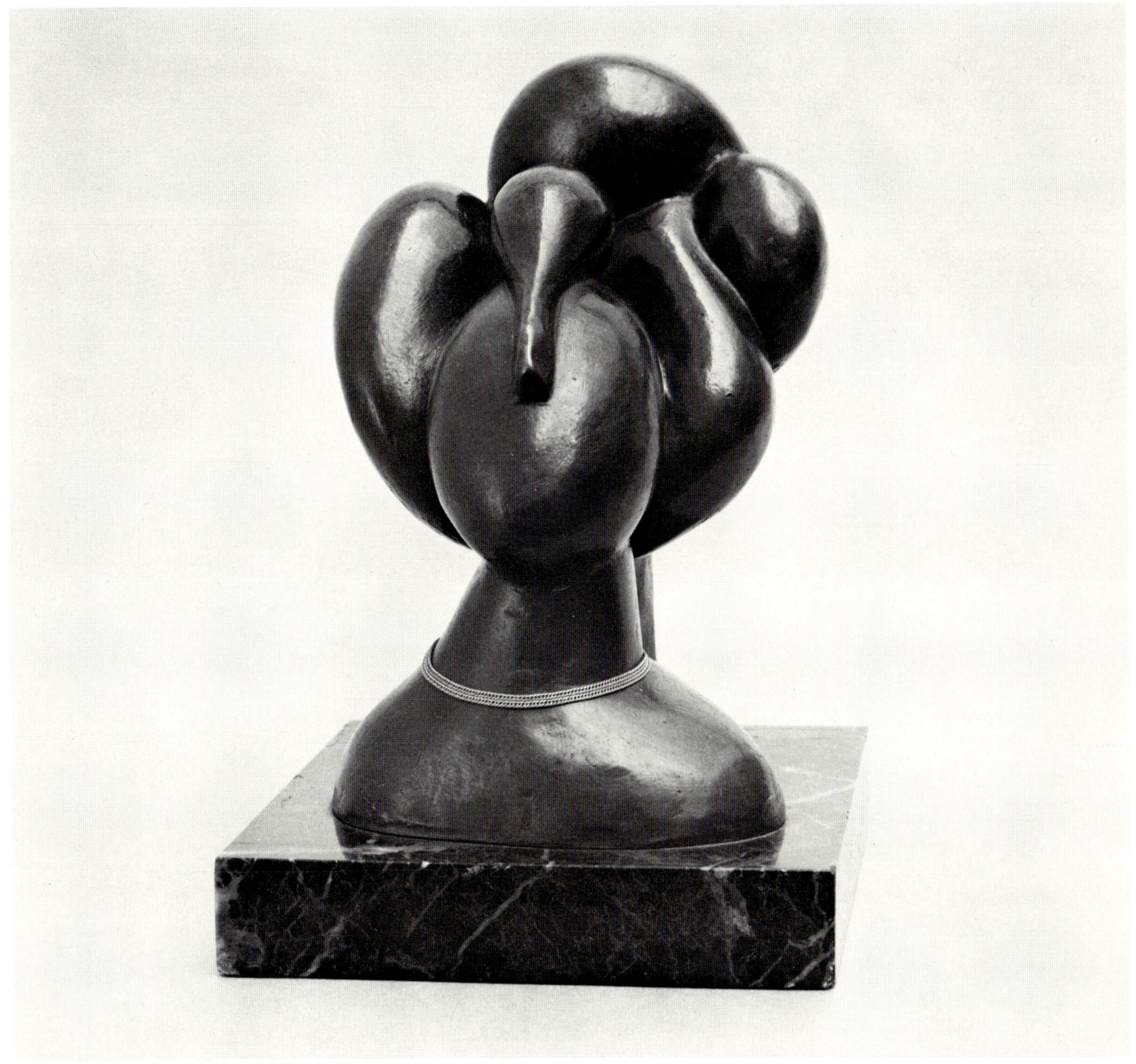

Venus in a Shell, I. 1930. 12¼″ h.

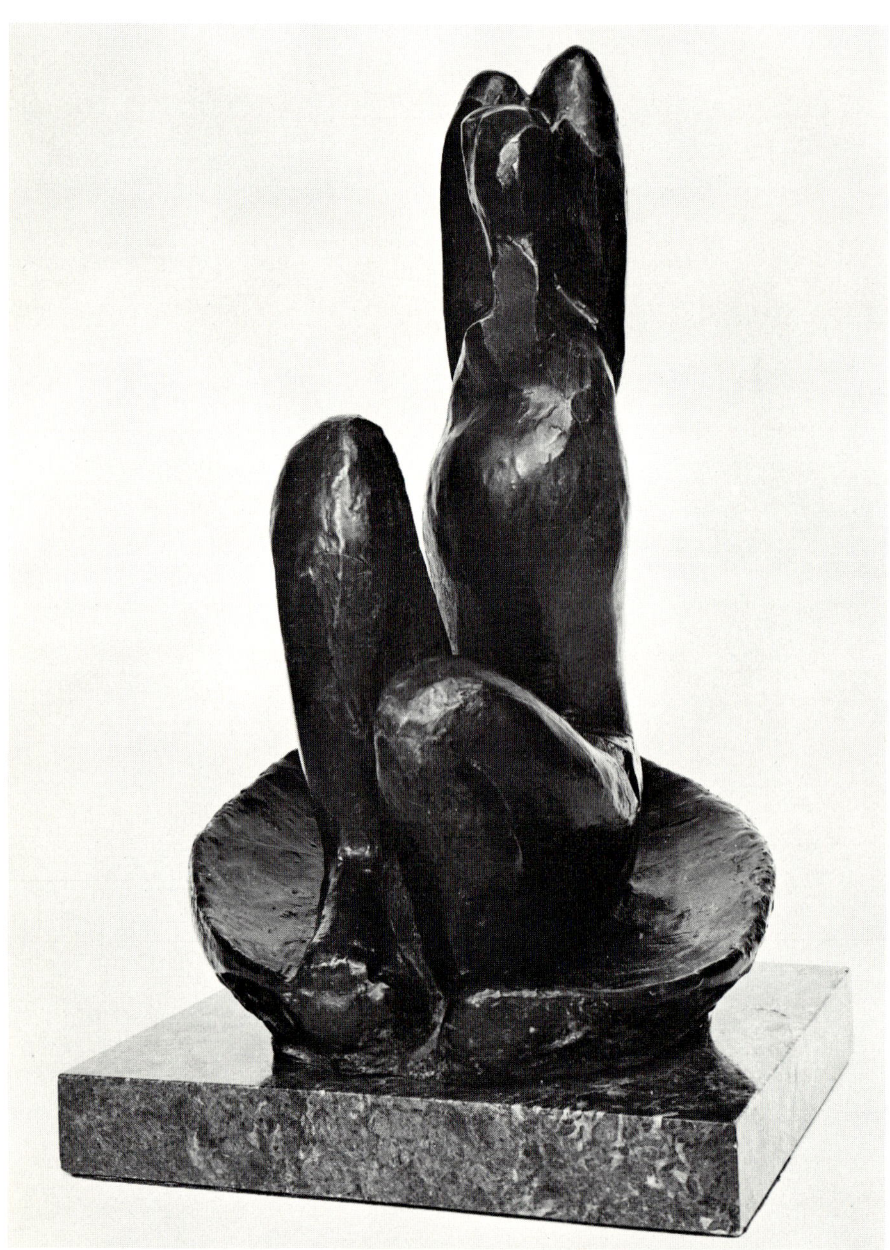

Standing Nude. 1930. Pencil

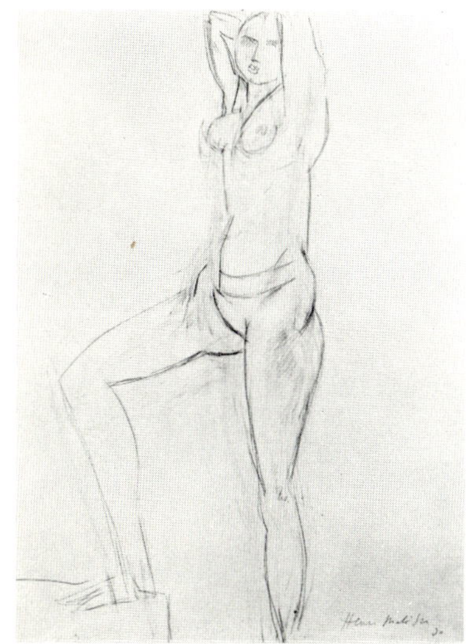

Venus in a Shell, II. 1932. $13\frac{3}{8}$" h.

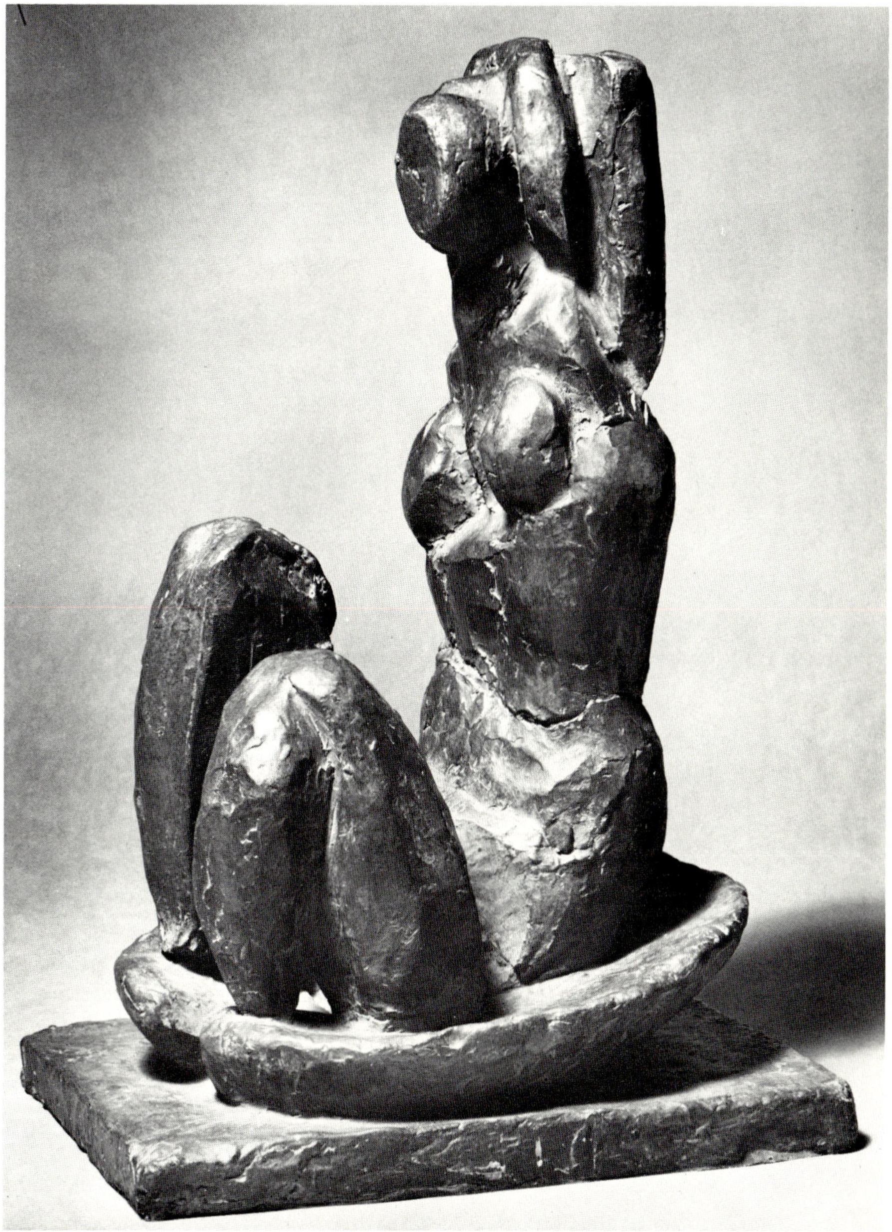

Study for *Christ*. 1949. Pen and ink and pencil

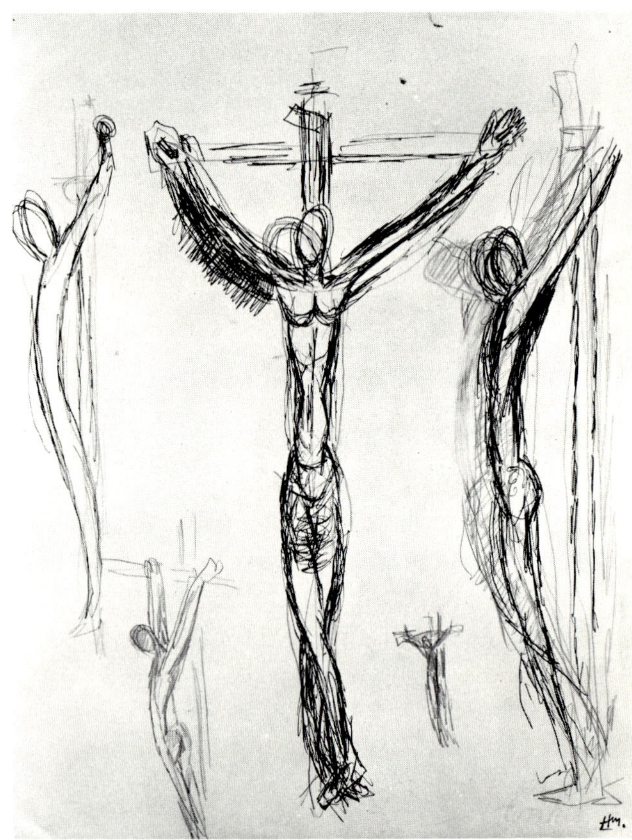

final version of *The Back* and *Tiari* in 1930. Inspired by a tropical flower that Matisse admired during a visit earlier that year to Tahiti, the latter work is a cluster of rounded forms. The simplified head is surmounted by such a weight of ovoid "petals," or "leaves," that a supporting wedge is needed at the back of the neck. To add a further curve to the composition of one of the ten casts, Matisse attached a necklace of fine chain. Jacques Lipchitz said of the sculpture: "The surfaces are almost neutral... the volumes are poetized to a sublime degree."[14] Within the next two years, he completed two versions of a seated nude probably derived from a Greek terra-cotta in the Louvre. *Venus in a Shell, I*, 1930, balances herself with raised knees in a bronze shell. In the second version, of 1932, the figure is more static and almost Cubist in construction.

Because of his concern with other projects, Matisse produced only three sculptures between 1932 and his death in 1954. After two serious operations in 1941, he spent much of his time in bed, working on drawings and the collages of cut paper that have become so influential in contemporary painting. In 1948 he began an intensive period of three years' work on the decoration of the Chapel of the Rosary for the Dominican Nuns of Vence, for which he provided designs for the architecture, stained-glass windows, and wall tiles. Although he adhered to no formal religious doctrine, this work absorbed him from a spiritual as well as an intellectual point of view. For the altar, he made a slender bronze crucifix.

The two final sculptures are the *Crouching Nude*, 1949, and *Standing Nude (Katia)*, 1950. The first has an almost primitive crudeness, with its arms and feet unfinished, and *Katia* is a last repetition of the woman with arms raised above her head. This time the upright figure is stretched almost in exaltation.

Matisse has been known principally through his paintings and drawings, and in recent years through the late cut-outs of painted paper. Throughout his career, however, he created some distinctively original and extraordinarily beautiful pieces, and his position as a sculptor is increasingly recognized.

Christ, Chapel of the Rosary for the Dominican Nuns of Vence. 1949. 13¾" h.

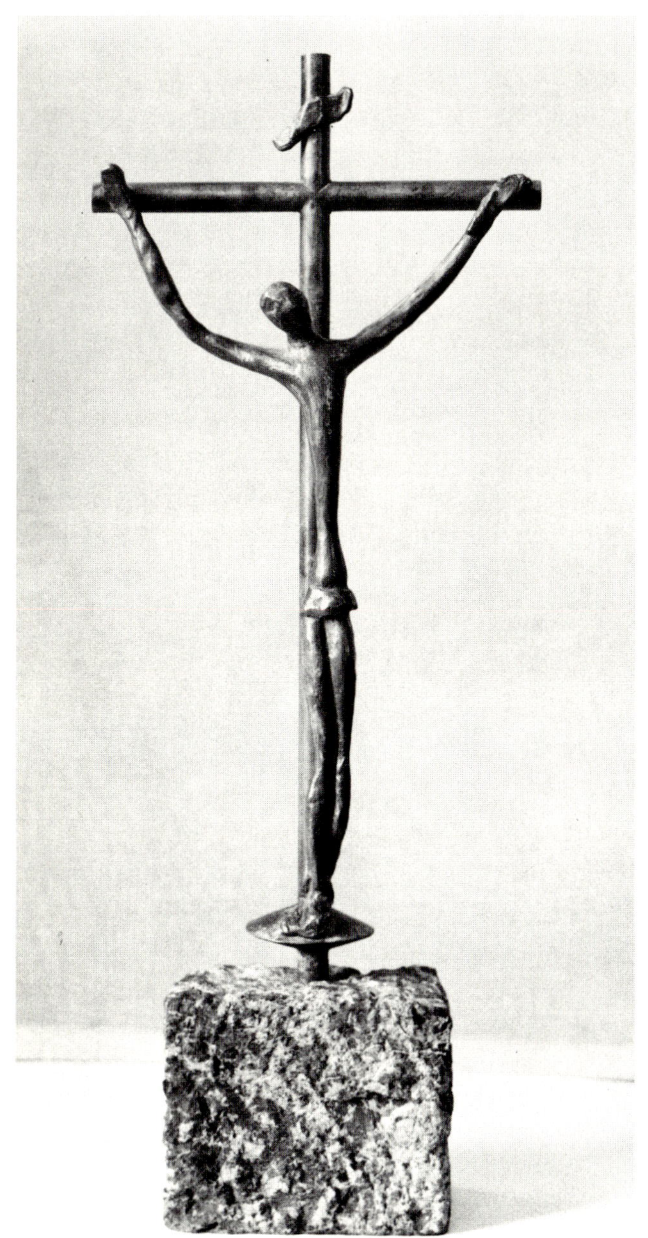

Crouching Nude. 1949. 10⅛" h.

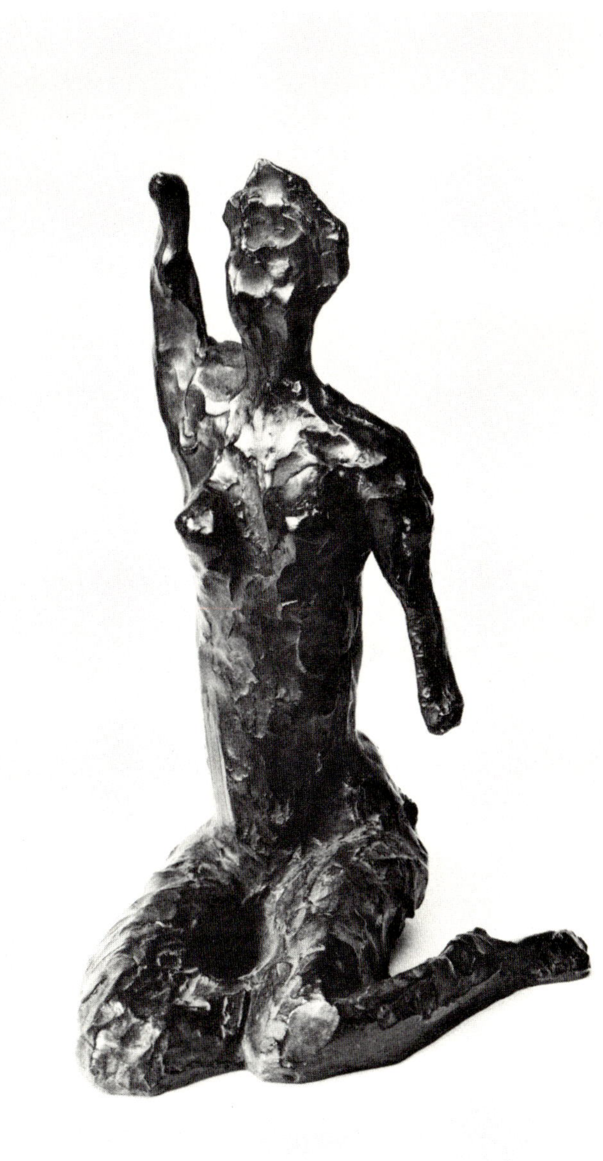

Notes

1. Conversation with Pierre Courthion, quoted in Jean Guichard-Meili, *Matisse.* New York: Frederick A. Praeger, 1967, p. 168. Translated from the French edition, Paris: Hazen, 1967.
2. Exhibitions of Matisse's sculpture, and those in which his sculpture plays an important part, are listed on page 48.
3. All of the sculptures are illustrated in the catalogue.
4. Albert E. Elsen, "The Sculpture of Matisse, Part I," *Artforum,* September 1968, p. 21. *The Sculpture of Henri Matisse,* a monograph by Albert E. Elsen, New York: Harry N. Abrams, 1972, grew out of the four-part series in *Artforum.*
5. Jean Puy, "Souvenirs," *Le Point,* vol. 4, no. 3, July 1939, p. 19.
6. Alfred H. Barr, Jr., *Matisse, His Art and His Public.* New York: The Museum of Modern Art, 1951, p. 100. With the painting *Still Life with a Plaster Figure* of 1906, Matisse began incorporating his sculptures into paintings. The *Reclining Nude, I* was to figure in at least eight oils. A list of Matisse's paintings that include images of his own sculpture appears on page 47.
7. This sculpture, in the Musée Matisse in Nice, is unavailable for the present exhibition because of its fragile condition.
8. Barr, *op. cit.,* p. 551.
9. Elsen, "The Sculpture of Matisse, Part II," *Artforum,* October 1968, p. 28.
10. Barr, *op. cit.,* p. 139.
11. Hilton Kramer, "Matisse as a Sculptor," *Bulletin* (Museum of Fine Arts, Boston), vol. 64, no. 336, 1966, p. 58.
12. Barr, *op. cit.,* p. 142.
13. George Besson, "Arrivée de Matisse à Nice," *Le Point,* vol. 4, no. 3, July 1939, p. 42.
14. Jacques Lipchitz, "Notes on Matisse as a Sculptor," *The Yale Literary Magazine,* Fall 1955, p. 12.

Standing Nude (Katia). 1950. $17\frac{3}{4}$" h.

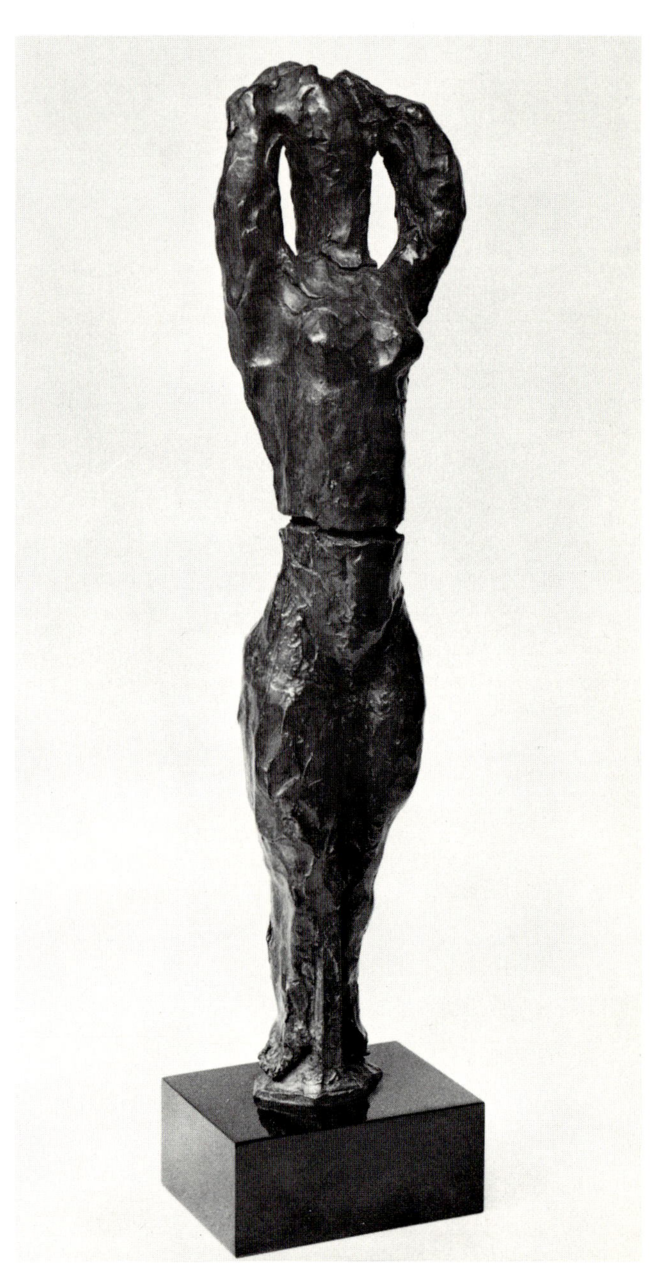

Sculptures by Matisse Seen in His Paintings

Madeleine, I. 1901
Still Life in Venetian Red. 1908. Pushkin Museum, Moscow

Copy after Puget's *Ecorché.* 1903
Interior with Eggplants. 1911. Musée de Peinture et de Sculpture, Grenoble
Still Life with Eggplants. 1911. Mrs. Bertram Smith, New York

Seated Nude with Arms on Head. 1904
The Red Studio. 1911. The Museum of Modern Art, New York

Woman Leaning on Her Hands. 1905
Still Life with Pelargonium. 1907. The Art Institute of Chicago

Standing Nude. 1906
Still Life with a Plaster Figure. 1906. Yale University Art Gallery, New Haven

Thorn Extractor. 1906
Still Life with Pelargonium. 1907. The Art Institute of Chicago

Reclining Nude, I. 1907
Sculpture and Persian Vase. 1908. National Gallery, Oslo
Goldfish. 1909 or 1910. Statens Museum for Kunst, Copenhagen
Still Life with Pewter Jug. 1910. The Hermitage, Leningrad
Goldfish and Sculpture. 1911. The Museum of Modern Art, New York
Goldfish. 1912. Barnes Foundation, Merion, Pennsylvania
Still Life with Ivy. ca. 1915. Private collection
The Music Lesson. 1917. Barnes Foundation, Merion, Pennsylvania
Studio at Nice. 1924. Mr. and Mrs. Paul Cushman, New York

Decorative Figure. 1908
The Pink Studio. 1911. Pushkin Museum, Moscow
The Red Studio. 1911. The Museum of Modern Art, New York
Piano Lesson. 1916. The Museum of Modern Art, New York

Small Crouching Nude with Arms. 1908
The Branch of Lilac. 1914. Private collection

Two Negresses. 1908
Fruit and Bronze. 1908. Pushkin Museum, Moscow

The Back, I. 1909
The Pink Studio. 1911. Pushkin Museum, Moscow

Jeannette, IV. 1910–13
The Red Studio. 1911. The Museum of Modern Art, New York

Jeannette, V. 1910–13. (?)
Still Life with a Bust. 1912. Barnes Foundation, Merion, Pennsylvania

Dance. 1911
Interior with Eggplants. 1911. Musée de Peinture et de Sculpture, Grenoble

List of Exhibitions

Exhibitions devoted primarily to sculpture are indicated by an asterisk. Others are listed to indicate early showings of sculpture, important retrospectives, and exhibitions in which the number of sculptures is considerable in relation to works in other mediums.

1904 Paris. Société du Salon d'Automne. Paintings, *2 plaster busts.*

1906 Paris. E. Druet Gallery. Mar. 19–Apr. 7. 55 paintings, graphics, *3 sculptures.*

1908 Paris. Société du Salon d'Automne. Paintings, *13 bronzes and plasters.*

1910–11 London. Grafton Galleries. Manet and the Post-Impressionists. Nov. 8–Jan. 15. Paintings, drawings, *7 bronzes.*

1912 *New York. Photo-Secession Gallery, "291." An Exhibition of Sculpture—the first in America—and Recent Drawings by Henri Matisse. Mar. 14–Apr. 6. *6 bronzes, 5 plasters, 1 terra-cotta,* 12 drawings.

London. Grafton Galleries. Second Post-Impressionist Exhibition. Oct. 19 paintings, drawings, prints, *7 sculptures.*

1913 New York. International Exhibition of Modern Art. "The Armory Show." Feb. 15–Mar. 15. 13 paintings, 3 drawings, *1 sculpture.*

Paris. Galerie Bernheim Jeune. Exposition Henri Matisse. Apr. 14–19. 11 paintings, *13 sculptures.*

1915 New York. Montross Gallery. Henri Matisse Exhibition. Jan. 20–Feb. 27. 74 works; *11 sculptures.*

1928 Venice. XVI Biennale. 33 works; *6 bronzes.*

1930 Berlin. Galerien Thannhauser. Henri Matisse. Retrospective. Feb. 15–Mar. 19. 265 works; *20 bronzes.* Catalogue.

1931 *New York. Brummer Gallery. Sculpture by Henri Matisse. Jan. 5–Feb. 7. *46 works;* 25 shown at Arts Club of Chicago, Mar. 13–28.

Basel. Kunsthalle. Henri-Matisse. Retrospective. Aug. 9–Sept. 15. 127 works; *15 bronzes.* Catalogue.

New York. Museum of Modern Art. Henri-Matisse. Retrospective. Nov. 3–Dec. 6. 162 works; *11 bronzes.* Catalogue.

1943 *New York. Buchholz Gallery. Bronzes by Degas, Matisse, Renoir. Oct. 19–Nov. 13. *12 works.*

1948 Philadelphia. Museum of Art. Henri Matisse. Retrospective. 271 works; *19 bronzes.* Catalogue.

1949 Lucerne. Musée des Beaux-Arts. Henri Matisse. Retrospective. July 9–Oct. 2. 308 works; *38 bronzes.* Catalogue.

1950 Paris. Maison de la Pensée Française. Henri Matisse: Chapelle, Peintures, Dessins, Sculptures. July 5–Sept. 24. 115 works; *51 bronzes.* Catalogue.

1951–52 New York. Museum of Modern Art. Henri Matisse. Retrospective. Nov. 13–Jan. 13. 145 works; *28 bronzes.* Catalogue. Also shown at Cleveland Museum of Art, Feb. 5–Mar. 16; Art Institute of Chicago, Apr. 1–May 4; San Francisco Museum of Art, May 22–July 6.

1953 *London. The Tate Gallery. An Exhibition of the Sculpture of Matisse and 3 Paintings with Studies. Jan. 9–Feb. 22. *48 bronzes.* Sponsored by the Arts Council of Great Britain. Catalogue, introduction by Jean Cassou.

*Copenhagen. Ny Carlsberg Glypotek. Henri Matisse, Skulpturer, Malerier, Farveklip. Nov. 6–Dec. 6. 55 works; *45 bronzes.* Organized by Mrs. Agnes Widlund, Stockholm. Catalogue, foreword by Haavard Rostrup, introduction by Jean Cassou. Most of the sculptures were subsequently shown at Kunstnernes Hus, Oslo, Feb. 20–Mar. 7, 1954; Museum Boymans, Rotterdam, Apr. 16–June 8, 1954; National Gallery of Canada, Ottawa, 1954; Museum of Fine Arts, Houston, Sept. 18–Oct. 16, 1955.

1954 *Stockholm. Nationalmuseum. Modern Utländsk Konst, Ur Svenska Privatsamlingar. Nov. 1 painting, 68 prints, *22 bronzes.* Catalogue.

Minneapolis. Institute of Arts. Matisse in Minneapolis. Nov. 16–Dec. 5. 26 works; *10 bronzes.*

1957 *Stockholm. Nationalmuseum. Henri Matisse: Apollon. Sept. 4–23. *43 bronzes.* Sponsored by the Association of Medical Students of Stockholm. Catalogue in Swedish and French. Subsequently shown as the Theodore Ahrenberg Collection, Skanska Museet, Lund, 1957; Helssingin Taidehalli, Helsinki, Dec. 10, 1957–Jan. 6, 1958; Musée des Beaux-Arts de Liège, May 3–July 31, 1958; Kunsthaus, Zurich, July 14–Aug. 12, 1959 (see separate entry); Konsthallen, Gothenburg, Mar. 16–Apr. 10, 1960.

1958 *New York. Fine Arts Associates. Henri Matisse: Sculpture, Drawings. Nov. 25–Dec. 20. *21 bronzes.* Catalogue.

1959 *Zurich. Kunsthaus. Henri Matisse: Das plastische Werk. The complete sculpture of Matisse, as well as drawings, graphics and collages, lent by the Ahrenberg Collection, Stockholm, the artist's and Swiss private collections. July 14–Aug. 12. 193 works; *67 bronzes, 1 carved wood.* Catalogue, introduction by Eduard Hüttinger.

1961 Albi. Musée Toulouse-Lautrec. Henri Matisse. Retrospective. July 11–Sept. 15. 181 works; *63 bronzes.* Catalogue.

1966 Los Angeles. UCLA Art Council and UCLA Art Galleries. Retrospective. Jan. 5–Feb. 27. 345 works; *47 bronzes.* Catalogue, text on sculpture by Herbert Read. Also shown at Art Institute of Chicago, Mar. 11–Apr. 24; Museum of Fine Arts, Boston, May 11–June 26.

1969 *London. Victor Waddington. Henri Matisse, Sculpture. June 12–July 12. *16 bronzes,* 11 lithographs. Catalogue, introduction by William Tucker.

1970 Paris. Grand Palais. Henri Matisse: Exposition du Centenaire. Apr. 21–Sept. 21. 277 works; *28 bronzes.* Catalogue, text by Pierre Schneider.

Catalogue of the Exhibition

Titles are given in English and French. In some cases, alternate titles are given. The dates of sculptures refer to the original version in clay or plaster. With some revisions, the dating is based on the catalogue of the exhibition *Henri Matisse: Das plastische Werk* at the Kunsthaus, Zurich, in 1959, which included sixty-eight sculptures. Dates for drawings are enclosed in parentheses when they do not appear on the works. In the dimensions, height precedes width and depth. Dimensions for drawings give sheet size, and for prints, composition size. Numbers in parentheses, beginning with (121), refer to the order of casting in bronze. Matisse bronzes are in editions of 10, with the exception of no. 1 (edition of 3) and no. 68 (edition of 5). Inscriptions are given for most sculptures. Two foundries were used, and most casts have a founder's stamp: "A. Bingen-Costenoble/Fondeurs, Paris," or "Cire/C. Valsuani/Perdue." The letters (NY), (M), or (B) indicate that a particular cast will be shown only in New York, Minneapolis, or Berkeley. All of the sculptures in the exhibition are illustrated in the catalogue on the pages indicated at the end of each entry. An asterisk indicates that a different cast from the one exhibited in New York is illustrated.

SCULPTURE

1 *Profile of a Woman (Profil de femme)*. 1894. Bronze medallion, 9⅝ inches diameter. (180 bis). "H. Matisse 94 / HM 0/3." Private collection. Page 8*

2 *Profile of a Woman (Profil de femme)*. 1894. Bronze medallion, 9⅝ inches diameter. (180). "HM 1/10." Private collection. Page 8

3 Copy after Barye's *Jaguar Devouring a Hare (Jaguar dévorant un lièvre d'après Barye)*. 1899–1901. Bronze, 9 x 22 x 9 inches. (144). "HM 9/10." Valsuani. Private collection. Page 8*

4 *Study of a Foot (Etude de pied)*. 1900. Bronze, 11¾ inches high. (152). "HM 7/10." Valsuani. Collection Jean Matisse, Paris. Page 8

5 *Bust of a Woman (Buste de femme; Buste ancien)*. 1900. Bronze, 24½ inches high. (155). "HM 5/10." Valsuani. Collection Pierre Matisse, New York. Page 8*

6 *The Serf (Le Serf)*. 1900–03. Bronze, 37⅜ inches high. (121). "Henri Matisse / Le Serf." Bingen-Costenoble. The Museum of Modern Art, New York, Mr. and Mrs. Sam Salz Fund. Page 10

7 *Horse (Le Cheval)*. 1901. Bronze, 6¾ inches high. (172). "HM 8." Valsuani. Collection Lewis Manilow, Chicago. Page 8

8 *Madeleine, I*. 1901. Bronze, 23⅜ inches high. (123). "Henri Matisse 00/10." Valsuani. Collection Mrs. M. Victor Leventritt, New York. (NY). "Henri Matisse 1/10." Valsuani. Private collection. (M, B). Page 11

9 *Madeleine, II*. 1903. Bronze, 23⅞ inches high. (153). "HM 5." Valsuani. Private collection. Page 11*

10 *Profile of a Child (Marguerite) (Profil d'enfant)*. 1903. Bronze, bas-relief, 5 x 3⅝ inches. (162). "HM 4/10." Private collection. Page 14*

11 Copy after Puget's *Ecorché (L'Ecorché d'après Puget)*. 1903. Bronze, 9 inches high. (182). "HM 2/10." Valsuani. Joseph H. Hirshhorn Collection. Page 8

12 *Seated Nude with Arms on Head (Nu assis, bras sur la tête)*. 1904. Bronze, 13⅞ inches high.

(141). "HM 4." Valsuani. Collection Mr. and Mrs. James S. Adams, New York. Page 12

13 *Upright Nude with Arched Back (Nu cambré)*. 1904. Bronze, 8⅞ inches high. (165). "HM 9/10." Valsuani. Collection Mrs. Melville J. Kolliner, Los Angeles. Page 13

14 *Head of a Child (Pierre Matisse) (Tête d'enfant, Pierre Matisse)*. 1905. Bronze, 6⅜ inches high. (138). "H Matisse 8/10." Collection Pierre Matisse, New York. Page 14

15 *Head of a Child (Pierre Manguin) (Tête d'enfant, Pierre Manguin)*. 1905. Bronze, 5⅛ inches high. (158). "7/10 HM." Valsuani. Collection Mr. and Mrs. Fritz Katz, Lake Success, New York. Page 14

16 *Rosette*. 1905. Bronze, 4¼ inches high. (188). "HM 5/10." Valsuani. Collection Jean Matisse, Paris. Page 15

17 *Woman Leaning on Her Hands (Femme appuyée sur les mains)*. 1905. Bronze, 5¼ x 9¾ x 5¼ inches. (124). "HM 2/10." Collection Mr. and Mrs. Edward M. M. Warburg, New York. (NY). "HM 5/10." The Cone Collection, The Baltimore Museum of Art. (M, B). Page 16*

18 *Reclining Figure with Chemise (Nu couché à la chemise)*. 1906. Bronze, 5½ x 11¾ x 6 inches. (127). "HM 5/10." Valsuani. The Baltimore Museum of Art, gift of Albert Lion. Page 18

19 *Small Head with Flat Nose (Petite tête au nez camus)*. 1906. Bronze, 6¼ inches high. (167). "HM 3." Valsuani. Private collection. Page 14

20 *Small Head with Upswept Hair (Petite tête au cheveux striés)*. 1906. Bronze, 4½ inches high. (170). "HM 5/10." Collection Dr. and Mrs. Harry Bakwin, New York. Page 14

21 *Head of a Young Girl (Marguerite) (Tête de fillette, Marguerite)*. 1906. Bronze, 6¼ inches high. (126). "Henri Matisse 5/10." Valsuani. The Cone Collection, The Baltimore Museum of Art. (NY). "9 Henri Matisse." Valsuani. Collection Frank Perls, Beverly Hills. (M, B). Page 14

22 *Standing Nude (Nu debout; Nu de fillette)*. 1906. Bronze, 19 inches high. (139). "HM 9." Valsuani. The Jeffrey H. Loria Collection. Page 17*

23 *Standing Nude, Arms on Head; Braced Nude (Nu debout, bras sur la tête; Nu campé)*. 1906. Bronze, 10⅜ inches high. (132). "Henri Matisse/10." Valsuani. Collection Mrs. Bertram Smith, New York. (NY). "Henri Matisse 4/10." Valsuani. The Philip H. and A. S. W. Rosenbach Foundation, Philadelphia. (M, B). Page 13

24 *Torso with Head (La Vie) (Torse avec tête, la vie)*. 1906. Bronze, 9⅛ inches high. (137). "Henri Matisse 9/10." The Metropolitan Museum of Art, New York, The Alfred Stieglitz Collection, 1949. (NY). "Henri Matisse 1/10." Private collection. (M, B). Page 13

25 *Thorn Extractor (Tireur d'épines)*. 1906. Bronze, 7½ inches high. (177). "3/10." Private collection. Page 15*

26 *Head of a Faun (Tête de faune)*. 1907. Bronze, 5½ inches high. (166). "HM 2/10." Valsuani. Collection Jean Matisse, Paris. Page 15

27 *Small Head with Comb (Petite tête au peigne; Petite tête)*. 1907. Bronze, 3¾ inches high. (136). "HM 7/10." The Cone Collection, Weatherspoon Art Gallery, The University of North Carolina at Greensboro. Page 14

28 *Head with Necklace (Tête au collier)*. 1907. Bronze, 5⅞ inches high. (130). "HM 7/10." Valsuani. Private collection, New York. (NY). "8/10 HM." The Cone Collection, The Baltimore Museum of Art. (M, B). Page 14*

29 *Reclining Nude, I (Nu couché, I; Aurore)*. 1907. Bronze, 13½ x 19¾ x 11¼ inches. (129). "Henri Matisse 7/10." The Museum of Modern Art, New York, acquired through the Lillie P. Bliss Bequest. (NY). "Henri Matisse 2/10." Bingen-Costenoble. Collection Mrs. Philip N. Lilienthal, Burlingame, California. (M, B). Page 19

30 *Seated Figure, Right Hand on Ground; Seated Nude (Nu assis, main droite à terre)*. 1908. Bronze, 7½ inches high. (133). "7/10 HM." Valsuani. The Museum of Modern Art, New York, Abby Aldrich Rockefeller Fund. Page 21

31 *Small Crouching Nude with Arms (Petit nu accroupi avec bras)*. 1908. Bronze, 6 inches high. (135). "5/10." Private collection. Page 21*

32 *Small Crouching Nude without an Arm (Petit nu accroupi sans bras)*. 1908. Bronze, 4¾ inches high. (134). "HM 7/10." The Cone Collection, Weatherspoon Art Gallery, The University of North Carolina at Greensboro. Page 21

33 *Small Crouching Torso (Petit torse accroupi)*. 1908. Bronze, 3⅛ inches high. (178). "HM 7." Collection Harry I. Caesar, Litchfield, Connecticut. (NY). "3/10." Private collection. (M, B). Page 21

34 *Decorative Figure (Figure décorative)*. 1908. Bronze, 28¾ inches high. (169). "HM 1908 / H'4." Valsuani. Joseph H. Hirshhorn Collection. Page 22

35 *Two Negresses (Deux Négresses)*. 1908. Bronze, 18½ inches high. (122). "Henri Matisse / HM 8/10." Collection Dr. and Mrs. Harry Bakwin, New York. Page 23

36 *Standing Nude (Nu debout)*. 1908. Bronze bas-relief, 9 x 4½ inches. (161). "HM 7/10." Private collection. Page 25*

37 *Torso without Arms or Head (Torse sans bras ni tête)*. 1909. Bronze, 9¾ inches high. (160). "HM 5." Joseph H. Hirshhorn Collection. Page 25*

38 *Seated Nude, Arm behind Her Back (Nu assis, bras derrière le dos)*. 1909. Bronze, 11⅝ inches high. (131). "HM 3/10." Bingen-Costenoble; Valsuani. Joseph H. Hirshhorn Collection. Page 22*

39 *The Back, I (Nu de dos, I)*. 1909. Bronze bas-relief, 74⅜ x 44¼ x 6½ inches. (146). "Henri Matisse / HM 2/10 / 1909." Valsuani. The Museum of Modern Art, New York, Mrs. Simon Guggenheim Fund. Page 26

40 *La Serpentine*. 1909. Bronze, 22¼ inches high. (142). "Henri Matisse / 1/10." The Museum of Modern Art, New York, gift of Abby Aldrich Rockefeller. (NY). "Henri Matisse 10." Private collection. (M, B). Page 24; cover

41 *Seated Nude (Olga) (Nu assis, Olga; Grand nu accroupi)*. 1910. Bronze, 17 inches high. (143). "HM 5." Valsuani. Collection Mr. and Mrs. Lee V. Eastman, New York. Page 21

42 *Jeannette, I* (Jeanne Vaderin, 1st state). 1910–13. Bronze, 13 inches high. (150). "0/10/HM." The Museum of Modern Art, New York, acquired through the Lillie P. Bliss Bequest. (NY). "HM 4."

Valsuani. Los Angeles County Museum of Art, presented by the Art Museum Council in memory of Mrs. Elmer C. Rigby. (M, B). Page 30

43 *Jeannette, II* (Jeanne Vaderin, 2nd state). 1910–13. Bronze, 10⅜ inches high. (149). "2/10 / HM." Valsuani. The Museum of Modern Art, New York, gift of Sidney Janis. (NY). "HM 5." Valsuani. Los Angeles County Museum of Art, presented by the Art Museum Council in memory of Mrs. Elmer C. Rigby. (M, B). Page 30

44 *Jeannette, III* (Jeanne Vaderin, 3rd state). 1910–13. Bronze, 23¾ inches high. (148). "5/10 / HM." The Museum of Modern Art, New York, acquired through the Lillie P. Bliss Bequest. (NY). "HM 4." Valsuani. Los Angeles County Museum of Art, presented by the Art Museum Council in memory of Mrs. Elmer C. Rigby. (M, B). Page 30

45 *Jeannette, IV* (Jeanne Vaderin, 4th state). 1910–13. Bronze, 24⅛ inches high. (151). "5/10 HM." Valsuani. The Museum of Modern Art, New York, acquired through the Lillie P. Bliss Bequest. (NY). "HM 4." Valsuani. Los Angeles County Museum of Art, presented by the Art Museum Council in memory of Mrs. Elmer C. Rigby. (M, B). Page 31

46 *Jeannette, V* (Jeanne Vaderin, 5th state). 1910–13. Bronze, 22⅞ inches high. (168). "5/10 HM." The Museum of Modern Art, New York, acquired through the Lillie P. Bliss Bequest. (NY). "HM 1/10." Valsuani. Los Angeles County Museum of Art, presented by the Art Museum Council in memory of Mrs. Elmer C. Rigby. (M, B). Page 31

47 *Dance (La Danse)*. 1911. Bronze, 16⅝ inches high. (176). "HM 1/10." Valsuani. Joseph H. Hirshhorn Collection. Page 20

48 *The Back, II (Nu de dos, II)*. 1913. Bronze bas-relief, 74½ x 47⅝ x 6 inches. (181). "Henri Matisse / HM / 2/10." The Museum of Modern Art, New York, Mrs. Simon Guggenheim Fund. Page 27

49 *Head of Marguerite (Tête de Marguerite)*. 1915. Bronze, 12⅝ inches high. (125). "HM 4/10." Valsuani. Collection Mr. and Mrs. Ralph F. Colin, New York. Page 32

50 *The Back, III (Nu de dos, III)*. 1916–17. Bronze bas-relief, 74½ x 44 x 6 inches. (145). "Henri M / HM / 1/10." Valsuani. The Museum of Modern Art, New York, Mrs. Simon Guggenheim Fund. Page 28

51 *Seated Nude Clasping Her Right Leg; Seated Venus (Nu assis, bras autour de la jambe droite; Vénus assise)*. 1918. Bronze, 9 inches high. (157). "HM 5/10." Valsuani. Collection Mr. and Mrs. Howard A. Weiss, Chicago. Page 33

52 *Venus; Crouching Venus (Vénus accroupie)*. ca. 1918. Bronze, 10¼ inches high. (156). "HM 6/10." Valsuani. The Cone Collection, The Baltimore Museum of Art. Page 33

53 *Reclining Nude with Bolster; Figure with Cushion (Nu couché au polochon)*. 1918. Bronze, 4¾ x 9½ x 4¼ inches. (128). "Henri Matisse 3/10." Valsuani. The Philip H. and A. S. W. Rosenbach Foundation, Philadelphia. Page 33*

54 *Large Seated Nude (Grand nu assis; Nu assis, bras sur la tête)*. 1923–25. Bronze, 33 inches high.

(159). Valsuani. Collection Nelson A. Rockefeller, New York. Page 34

55 *Small Nude in an Armchair (Petit nu au canapé)*. 1924. Bronze, 9½ inches high. (184). "HM 0/10." Valsuani. Private collection. Page 35*

56 *Henriette, I*. 1925. Bronze, 11½ inches high. (185). "HM 9/10." Valsuani. Collection Mr. and Mrs. Nathan Cummings, New York. (NY). "HM 5/10." Valsuani. Private collection. (M, B). Page 36

57 *Henriette, II*. 1927. Bronze, 12⅝ inches high. (140). "6/10 HM." Valsuani. San Francisco Museum of Art, bequest of Harriet Lane Levy. Page 36

58 *Reclining Nude, II (Nu couché, II)*. 1927. Bronze, 11½ x 20¼ x 6½ inches. (179). "HM 2/10." Valsuani. Florene M. Schoenborn and Samuel A. Marx Collection, New York. (NY). "8." Valsuani. The Minneapolis Institute of Arts, gift of the Dayton-Hudson Corporation. (M). "5/10 HM." Valsuani. Collection Mr. and Mrs. Sidney F. Brody, Los Angeles. (B). Page 38

59 *Reclining Nude, III (Nu couché, III)*. 1929. Bronze, 7¼ x 18¼ x 5¼ inches. (154). "HM 7/10." Joseph H. Hirshhorn Collection. Page 39

60 *Henriette, III (Tête souriante)*. 1929. Bronze, 15¾ inches high. (163). "HM 6." Valsuani. Joseph H. Hirshhorn Collection. Page 37

61 *Small Torso (Petit torse)*. 1929. Bronze, 3½ inches high. (174). "9." Collection Mr. and Mrs. Benjamin Weiss, New York. Page 40

62 *Small Thin Torso (Petit torse mince)*. 1929. Bronze, 3 inches high. (171). "HM 3." Valsuani. Collection Jean Matisse, Paris. Page 40

63 *The Back, IV (Nu de dos, IV)*. 1930. Bronze bas-relief, 74½ x 44 x 6 inches. (147). Valsuani. The Museum of Modern Art, New York, Mrs. Simon Guggenheim Fund. Page 29

64 *Tiari (Le Tiaré)*. 1930. Bronze, 8 inches high. (175). "2/10 / HM." Valsuani. The Museum of Modern Art, New York, A. Conger Goodyear Fund. (NY). *Tiari (with Necklace)*. "HM 1/10." Valsuani. The Cone Collection, The Baltimore Museum of Art. (NY, M, B). Pages 40, 41

65 *Venus in a Shell, I (Vénus à la coquille, I)*. 1930. Bronze, 12¼ inches high. (173). "HM 2/10." Valsuani. The Museum of Modern Art, New York, gift of Charles Simon. Page 42

66 *Venus in a Shell, II (Vénus à la coquille, II)*. 1932. Bronze, 13⅜ inches high. (183). "HM 3/10." Valsuani. Joseph H. Hirshhorn Collection. Page 43

67 *Crouching Nude; Small Crouching Figure; Seated Nude (Nu accroupi; Petit figure accroupi; Nu assis)*. 1949. Bronze, 10⅛ inches high. (187). "HM 8/10." Valsuani. Collection Mr. and Mrs. Walter Bareiss, Greenwich, Connecticut. Page 45*

68 *Christ (Le Christ), Chapel of the Rosary for the Dominican Nuns of Vence (Altar Crucifix)*. 1949. Bronze, 13¾ inches high (height of cross 16⅛ inches). (189). "HM 0/1." Valsuani. Collection Jean Matisse, Paris. Page 45

69 *Standing Nude (Katia) (Nu debout, Katia, dit la taille cassée)*. 1950. Bronze, 17¾ inches high. (186). "4/10." Valsuani. Collection Mr. and Mrs. Allan D. Emil, New York. (NY). "HM 3/10."

Valsuani. Collection Mr. and Mrs. Paul Kantor, Malibu, California. (M, B). Page 46*

DRAWINGS

70 Study for *Madeleine*. (ca. 1901). Pencil, 11¾ x 9¼ inches. The Museum of Modern Art, New York, gift of Mr. and Mrs. Pierre Matisse in honor and memory of M. Victor Leventritt. Page 10

71 *Nude Study (Académie de femme)*. (ca. 1903). Charcoal, 13 x 8½ inches. Private collection

72 *Woman Leaning on Her Hands (Femme appuyée sur les mains)*. (1905). Pen and ink, 6⅝ x 8¾ inches. Collection Jean Matisse, Paris

73 *The Artist's Daughter, Marguerite*. (ca. 1905). Pen and ink, 15⅝ x 20½ inches. Private collection, Toronto

74 *Marguerite Reading*. (ca. 1906). Pen and ink, 15⅝ x 20½ inches. The Museum of Modern Art, New York, acquired through the Lillie P. Bliss Bequest, 1953

75 *Reclining Woman, I* (study for the sculpture *Reclining Figure with Chemise*). (1906). Pen and ink, 6¾ x 12¼ inches. The Museum of Modern Art, New York, extended loan from the Joan and Lester Avnet Collection

76 *Reclining Woman, II* (study for the sculpture *Reclining Figure with Chemise*). (1906). Pen and ink, 6¾ x 8¾ inches. The Museum of Modern Art, New York, extended loan from the Joan and Lester Avnet Collection. Page 18

77 *Reclining Woman, III* (study for the sculpture *Reclining Figure with Chemise*). (1906). Pen and ink, 6⅞ x 8⅞ inches. The Museum of Modern Art, New York, extended loan from the Joan and Lester Avnet Collection

78 *Nude with Pipes*. 1906. Pen and ink, 18 x 23¾ inches. Collection Mr. and Mrs. Richard S. Davis, London. (NY)

79 *Nude Study* (study for *The Back, I*). (ca. 1907). Pen and ink, 10½ x 8⅝ inches. The Museum of Modern Art, New York, Carol Buttenwieser Loeb Memorial Fund

80 Study after the painting *Dance* (first version). (ca. 1909). Pencil, 8⅝ x 13⅞ inches. The Museum of Modern Art, New York, gift of Pierre Matisse

81 *Seated Model Clasping Knee*. 1909. Reed pen and ink, 11⅝ x 9¼ inches. The Art Institute of Chicago, gift of Mrs. Emily Crane Chadbourne. Page 33

82 *Girl with Tulips (Jeanne Vaderin)*. (1910). Charcoal on buff paper, 28½ x 23 inches. The Museum of Modern Art, New York, acquired through the Lillie P. Bliss Bequest

83 *Crouching Nude*. (1912). Pen and ink, 12½ x 8⅞ inches. The Metropolitan Museum of Art, New York, The Alfred Stieglitz Collection, 1949. (NY). Page 21

84 Study for *The Back, II*. (ca. 1913). Pen and ink, 8 x 6¼ inches. The Museum of Modern Art, New York, gift of Pierre Matisse. Page 26

85 *Reclining Nude with Bolster*. (1918). Pencil, 11 x 15 inches. Private collection

86 Study for the painting *Odalisque*. (ca. 1925). Charcoal, 16 x 20¼ inches. The Museum of Modern Art, New York, Katherine S. Dreier Bequest

87 *Standing Nude.* 1930. Pencil, 12¾ x 9½ inches. Robert Elkon Gallery, New York. Page 43

88 Study for *Christ, Chapel of the Rosary for the Dominican Nuns of Vence.* (1949). Pen and ink and pencil, 17 x 13 inches. Musée Matisse, Nice. Page 44

PRINTS

89 *Half-Length Nude, Eyes Cast Down.* (1906). Transfer lithograph, 17⅝ x 9½ inches. The Museum of Modern Art, New York, given anonymously in memory of Leo and Nina Stein. Page 17

90 *Day (Female Nude, Arms behind Head) (Le Jour).* (1922). Lithograph, 9⅞ x 11 inches. "Henri Matisse 5/50/HM." The Cone Collection, The Baltimore Museum of Art. (NY). "Henri Matisse 6/50." Stanford University Museum of Art, Stanford, California, gift of Mrs. Michael Stein. (M, B). Page 35

91 *Night (La Nuit).* (1922). Lithograph, 9⅞ x 11⅝ inches. "Henri Matisse / épreuve d'artiste 3/10." Private collection, New York. (NY)

92 *Seated Nude with Arms Raised.* (1924). Lithograph, 24¼ x 18⅜ inches. The Museum of Modern Art, New York, gift of Abby Aldrich Rockefeller

CERAMIC

93 *Reclining Nude.* (1907). Ceramic tile, 4 x 5 inches. Collection Joy S. Weber, Great Neck, New York

Photograph Credits

Courtesy Art Institute of Chicago, 33 top left
Courtesy Baltimore Museum of Art, 14 center left, 18, 33 bottom left, 35 top
Rudolph Burckhardt, New York, 42
Cauvin, Paris, 8 top center, 8 center, 8 top right, 14 top left, 15 top right, 15 bottom right, 25 bottom, 40 top left, 45 left
Jonas Dorydenas, Chicago, 33 top right
Claude Frossard, Le Canet, 44
James Mathews, New York, 10 right, 14 top center, back cover
Courtesy Metropolitan Museum of Art, New York, 13 center
O. E. Nelson, New York, 8 bottom right, 20, 22 left, 37, 39, 43 right
Rolf Petersen, New York, 13 left, 40 right, 41
Eric Pollitzer, Garden City Park, N.Y., 26 right
Edward Steichen, frontispiece
Adolph Studly, Pennsburg, Pa., 8 bottom left, 11 left, 11 right, 12, 13 right, 14 center, 14 center right, 14 bottom left, 14 bottom right, 15 left, 16, 17 left, 21 top left, 21 top right, 21 bottom right, 22 right, 23, 25 top, 27, 32, 33 bottom right, 34, 36 right, 38 top, 38 bottom, 40 bottom left
Soichi Sunami, New York, front cover, 10 left, 17 right, 19, 21 top center, 21 bottom center, 24, 26 left, 28, 29, 30 top left, 30 bottom left, 30 right, 31 left, 31 right
Cathy Swanson, Greensboro, N. C., 21 bottom left
Charles Uht, New York, 18 top
Malcolm Varon, New York, 14 top right, 36 left
Etienne Bertrand Weill, Courbevoie, 8 center left